CHAN HEART, CHAN ART

Venerable Master Hsing Yun

Translated and edited by
Pey-Rong Lee and Dana Dunlap

Buddha's Light Publishing
3456 S. Glenmark Drive
Hacienda Heights, CA 91745, U.S.A.
Tel: (626) 923-5144
Fax: (626) 923-5145
E-mail: info@blpusa.com
Website: www.blpusa.com

Venerable Master Hsing Yun
Translated and edited by Pey-Rong Lee and Dana Dunlap
Paintings by Gao Ertai and Pu Xiaoyu
Cover design by Dung Trieu and Fo Guang Yuan Art Gallery

ISBN-10: 1-932293-23-X
ISBN-13: 978-1-932293-23-4

Library of Congress Cataloging-in-Publication Data

Xingyun, da shi.
  Chan heart, Chan art / Hsing Yun ; translated and edited by Pey-Rong Lee and Dana Dunlap.
     p. cm.
Translations of selections from Chinese.
Includes bibliographical references.
ISBN 1-932293-23-X (pbk. : alk. paper)
1. Koan. 2. Zen Buddhism--Anecdotes. 3. Priests, Zen--China--Art. 4. Fo Guang Shan Buddhist Order.
I. Lee, Pey-Rong. II. Dunlap, Dana. III. Title.

BQ9800.F6392X55426 2007
294.3'432--dc22

2006102399

Contents

What Is Chan?

Chan is a world that cannot be expressed through words. However, it is said, "The top of the wondrous peak cannot be transmitted with words. The second peak barely allows words." Although the state of Chan cannot be explained with words, yet if we do not speak at all, how can the average person appreciate Chan's profound meaning? Therefore, Chan patriarchs and virtuous practitioners throughout the ages have diligently taught Chan in the gently nagging way of a little old lady. Consequently, many gongans and recorded sayings have been passed down to later generations. To this day, Buddhist disciples still talk about Chan with great enthusiasm.

Chan is a world that cannot be seen nor heard. Nevertheless, as the Sixth Patriarch Huineng said, "The Dharma is in the world; it is not apart from worldly awareness. Seeking bodhi apart from the world is like looking for horns on a rabbit." If the people living in this world depart from the worldly senses of seeing, hearing, feeling, and understanding, how can they seek and attain the path of Chan teachings? Bhiksu Bei, of the Buddha's time, used the sound of his moving and beautiful voice to prevent King Prasenajit from executing his plan to attack a neighboring country. When India's Asvaghosa Bodhisattva performed "Rastrapala," an epic poem that he had composed, five hundred princes of the Pataliputra clan awakened to the Way and became monks. Wu Chengen's *Journey to the West* was based on the story of Xuanzang's travels to India. Transmitted over six centuries and deep with symbolic meaning, it appealed to both the sophisticated and the average person. D.T. Suzuki used prajna words to propagate the Dharma, which resonated with numerous Westerners. All these methods of purifying the six senses move a deep spiritual part of the heart and awaken our inherent Buddha nature. How can they not be manifestations of the principles of Chan?

Therefore, what is Chan? Chan is the essence of our true intrinsic nature. Chan is our original face. Chan is an inexhaustible treasure. Chan is the artistic life. Chan contains the universal characteristics of time and space. Chan contains the equality of human existence. Chan contains the humorous quality of wisdom. Chan contains the model of dignity. Chan is like a flower; it enriches the colors in life. Chan is like a pinch of salt; it adds flavor to this world. Chan is like a painting; it can beautify the environment. Chan is like a drop of water; it can nourish the body and mind. Chan is not limited by any form. With Chan, we can recognize the original nature of prajna-wisdom. With Chan, we can be taken to an even higher realm.

For the sake of allowing others to understand the wondrous way of Chan, I accepted an invitation in 1986 from Kaohsiung's evening newspaper to write a special column with *Hsing Yun's Chan Talk* as the subject. I took ancient and modern Chan histories that were full of meaning and interest and made them available to the public. In all, I wrote over five hundred consecutive columns. Then, the evening newspaper ceased publication. Since the management at China Television System (CTS) held me in high regard, they hoped I would record a program based upon *Hsing Yun's Chan Talk*. I joyfully consented. At CTS, we broadcast several hundred episodes. Subsequently, North America's satellite television station also requested permission to broadcast it for the enjoyment of the local Chinese community.

Later, Peter Lang Publishing, Inc. North America published the English translation of my Chan stories. Fo Guang Cultural Enterprise Co., Ltd. also issued a Chinese and Chinese-English edition of the Chan stories. In 1992, in response to readers' requests, the Lianjing Publishing Company published a book compiled from a series of articles, *Hsing Yun's Chan Talk*, that Mr. Yao Jiayan published in the *Economic*

Daily News for over a year. Crown Publishing Company also came forward and requested permission to print *Hsing Yun's Chan Talk*. It is really deeply gratifying to me to see the loving attention that such a small volume of Chan stories has received from everyone. It is evident that what the people of the world today urgently need is to lead a life flavored with Chan.

In 1993, the well-known painters from Mainland China, Gao Ertai and his wife, Pu Xiaoyu, came to the United States. Mr. Gao Ertai learned painting as a child from his father and later studied under Lu Fengzi, Wu Shuyang, Yan Wenliang, Lu Sibai, and other famous painters. By combining the specialties of these masters, he melded Chinese and western painting techniques to create his own path, one not bound by any single style. At a young age, he was already famous, and his extensive reading and study enriched the content of his paintings. He then spent more than ten years in the Dunhuang Caves copying authentic works from the various dynasties, during which time his artistic skill gradually reached an exalted state. In addition to his painting, research, and teaching, he has also written numerous literary compositions. This world-renowned authority on aesthetics was honored, in 1986, as a state expert with distinguished contributions to his field by the Mainland's Chinese National Science Council.

His wife, Pu Xiaoyu, is not only a painter, but also a noted woman of letters. Her paintings, modeled after ancient styles, were on display at the Beijing Museum for some time. In 1993, her large masterpiece, "Avalokitesvara Bodhisattva of a Thousand Hands and Eyes," was displayed at Hong Kong City Hall and it received wide acclaim. Husband and wife share their interests as well as a deep commitment to one another. During their stay at Hsi Lai Temple, they used the content of *Hsing Yun's Chan Talk* as material for one hundred paintings. At the end of 1995, these works were exhibited for six months each at Taipei Fo Guang Yuan Art Gallery and Tainan Fo Guang Yuan Art Gallery, garnering a tide of distinguished reviews.

It is said, "The fragrance of a flower does not depend on its strength; why does an elegant room need to be big?" With a Chan mind, at no time and no moment is the pure land not manifesting before us. During the period that it flourished in China, Chan was expressed through the tea ceremony, flower arrangement, calligraphy, and swordsmanship. After it was transmitted to Japan, it was, instead, gradually losing ground in its native land and becoming the culture of others. Only Chan painting has never declined in China. Every generation has had new creativity. Gao Ertai's and Pu Xiaoyu's one hundred Chan paintings are true to life; the mood is serene and profound. We can say that they follow in the tradition of "The Sixteen Arhats" by Chanyue of the Tang Dynasty, "The Second Patriarch in Contemplation" by Shi Ke of the Five Dynasties, "The Sixth Patriarch Cutting Bamboo" by Liang Kai of the Southern Song Dynasty, "Hanshan and Shide" by Yintuoluo of the Yuan Dynasty, and other masterpieces, placing them among the most outstanding representatives of modern Chinese painting.

Observing people today, we can see that life's instability and chaos has caused anxiety, nervousness, and many other illnesses. However, the way of Chan has the greatest power to calm and stabilize the body and mind. Chan painting has the far-reaching effect of educating and bringing joy. Therefore, Fo Guang Cultural Enterprise Co., Ltd. is pairing Gao Ertai's and Pu Xiaoyu's one hundred paintings with my *Hsing Yun's Chan Talk* and publishing a book entitled *Chan Heart, Chan Art* to universally benefit society and its people. I feel its profound significance. Therefore, it is with joy that I write this preface.

Hsing Yun
1996, September
Fo Guang Shan

Foreword by the Artist

Xiaoyu and I painted these one hundred Chan paintings three years ago in Los Angeles at the request of Venerable Master Hsing Yun. When we first arrived in the United States, we had no family or friends, and not so much as a single penny. We were extremely grateful to Venerable Master Hsing Yun for providing us with an opportunity to earn our own living, allowing us to pave the way for a new life through our own efforts. At the time, we had two opportunities: one was to go to Harvard University as visiting scholars; the other was to go to Hsi Lai Temple to work on these paintings. We chose the latter. This first choice we made upon initially arriving in the United States determined our life's course for many years afterwards.

Out of gratitude to Venerable Master Hsing Yun, we worked extremely hard night and day, completing these one hundred paintings within half a year. During this time, because several publications were urgently asking for my manuscripts, I had no choice but to spend a great deal of time on them. Therefore, these paintings are mostly Xiaoyu's own compositions. She worked at Beijing Capital Museum for ten years copying ancient paintings, which is reflected in the strong traditional aura of these paintings.

Although the specifications and dimensions of the one hundred paintings are the same, each one has an independent theme. For this reason, we dedicated ourselves to giving the appearance of each character distinctive features, and did our very best not to make them similar. Avoiding duplication in one hundred paintings with one hundred compositions and hundreds of characters is really not easy. Particularly since monastics wear identical attire, only in the characteristics of the facial features and expressions could we seek variation. The degree of difficulty was even greater when conforming to the laws of human anatomy because we could only seek variation within the scope of artistic composition and proportion. If the readers can see in these one hundred paintings that every composition is different and the appearance of every character is distinct, then we will feel deeply contented.

There is a tradition in Chinese portrait painting that seeks to "accomplish social education and advocate human ethics." Frequently, it transforms words into a concrete and tangible form. For the two of us, the process of painting these works was propagating the Dharma as well as studying the Dharma. The source for the subject matter of these paintings is the four-volume *Hsing Yun's Chan Talk*. These four books not only present the vast wisdom of ancient Chan masters, but also the profound wisdom of Venerable Master Hsing Yun. Passing them on to the reader with the paintbrush is also a kind of meritorious deed. It is with this spirit that we offer all of these paintings to the readers.

The verses inscribed on the paintings were provided by Hsi Lai Temple and are not our work. We wish to make this clear and do not dare claim credit for them.

Gao Ertai
March 23, 1996
New Jersey

Translator's Introduction

All Buddhist teachings begin with a teacher and a student, and the instruction Venerable Master Hsing Yun offers us in this collection of Chan stories between masters and disciples is no exception. These are stories about self-awakenings: Chan masters who awakened to the Buddha's truth through the cultivation of their minds, and in turn, inspired countless students to practice Chan. The literature behind these teachings flows directly from the old masters' metaphors of the Buddha's realization, and is not necessarily history as conventionally conceived. Like all human experience, the history of Chan is mostly unrecorded in books. The true significance of these stories lies not in the events of the past, but in their effect on the students of the Way.

Chan was rooted in China by Bodhidharma, who traveled from India in the sixth century, and was then carried eastward to Japan in the twelfth century. By our worldly understanding, the Chan sages lived in a time and context so far removed from our own experience that we risk dismissing their wisdom outright, yet Chan is no less relevant today than it was in ancient China. It remains important precisely because the enlightenment of the historical Buddha and his Chan descendants does not depend on external cultural or social conditions so much as upon the state of the mind within us.

The Chan mind, the masters teach us, cannot be sought outside. Where then, can we find the mind? Venerable Master Hsing Yun recounts an encounter between Chan Master Nanyue Huairang and his teacher Songshan An to break through this very point:

> One day, Chan Master Nanyue Huairang of the Tang Dynasty paid a visit to Chan Master Songshan An and asked him, "What is the meaning of the patriarch coming to the West?"
> Songshan An asked in return, "Why don't you ask yourself?"
> Huairang then asked, "What is the meaning of self?"
> Songshan An replied, "Pure contemplation and wondrous function."
> Huairang inquired, "What is the wondrous function?"
> Chan Master An instructed him by opening and closing his eyes. At that moment, Huairang had a great awakening.

It is our physical eyes which perform the actions of opening and closing, but it is our true mind which gives the commands. At every moment, our true mind is not separate from us; most of the time, we obscure it or ignore it. What we must do to become aware of the mind is to examine and investigate it directly.

Chan Heart, Chan Art is a volume that attempts to penetrate to the very heart of Chan by directly demonstrating how the Chan life is as relevant to the casual reader as to the practitioner. Venerable Master Hsing Yun's approach is to let the Chan tradition speak for itself. In our translation, Dana and I have respected the Master's style of teaching by preserving the essential spirit of his words in order to fully capture the "flavor of Chan." He is the teacher and we are the students. For this reason, we have avoided providing our own interpretations and have, instead, allowed our translation to flow in the current of his words. The supplementary material appended to the stories is aimed at enriching the experiences of the readers and guiding them towards a deeper understanding of Chan. The section of explanatory notes explains key Buddhist terms, cultural references, and the layers of meaning alluded to in the original Chinese text. The biographical section provides a historical context to the lives of the notable Chan teachers and students who appear in the book.

In the last two years, working with Dana has profoundly deepened my awareness of cultivating the mind through translation. From moment to moment, he manifested Chan through the simple acts of listening to others and respecting others. For Dana, the experience of translating the Chan exchanges between masters and students was just another opportunity to speak Chan words, hear Chan sounds, do Chan deeds, and cultivate the Chan mind. It was by his example that the seeds of the Buddha's teachings began to take root in my life.

It can be said that the Buddha wanted us to reflect on the fact that we do not have forever to cultivate the mind. The same thing is true of Chan practice. It is not practice; it is your life in every moment. May you experience the living heart of Chan and awaken to your own true Chan mind.

Pey-Rong Lee

Acknowledgments

Chan Heart, Chan Art has benefited from the harmonious effort of many people, and we wish to thank them for standing behind this project from inception to completion. Venerable Tzu Jung, Chief Executive of the Fo Guang Shan International Translation Center, and Venerable Hui Chi, the abbot of Hsi Lai Temple, provided the encouragement and leadership to sustain our work. We are very grateful to Venerable Yi Chao and Venerable Miao Hsi, the directors of the Fo Guang Shan Translation Center and Buddha's Light Publishing, for guiding this book through the stages of translation and publication.

Acknowledgment is due to Pey-Rong Lee and Dana Dunlap for undertaking the immense work which was necessary to complete *Chan Heart, Chan Art*. The dedication with which they meticulously translated and edited the stories allows us to share these one hundred tales of eminent Chan teachers with others.

Many volunteers willingly contributed their time, knowledge, and energy in order to bring *Chan Heart, Chan Art* to fruition. None of this would have been possible without the support of Mu-Tzen Hsu, whose careful research on the Chan masters and instruction on the Buddha's teachings greatly improved successive drafts of the manuscript. Franc Shelton generously donated his time, translating the stories with Pey-Rong Lee during the earliest stages of the project. With regard to translation of the Chinese language, we humbly thank Shih Chen Ma, You Mei-Chen Lee, and Kevin Hsyeh for patiently offering assistance and advice. Venerable Chueh Duo and Emily Anderson were valuable resources on the Japanese Zen masters who appear throughout this book. We would also like to express our appreciation to Venerable Man Jen, Louvenia Ortega, Mike Hocutt, Diana Hocutt, Scott Hocutt, and Edmond Chang for proofreading and providing useful suggestions on the manuscript as a whole. Dung Trieu designed and arranged the book in its final form.

Finally, our special thanks go to the Fo Guang Yuan Art Gallery in Taiwan for supplying the Chan artwork beautifully painted by Gao Ertai and Pu Xiaoyu.

May all sentient beings benefit.

禅話

禅画

Hoe the Weeds, Chop the Snake

A student monk went to the temple of Chan Master Zhichang to study.

Chan Master Zhichang was hoeing weeds. Just then, a snake slithered out from among the weeds. The Chan Master raised his hoe and chopped.

The student monk said very disapprovingly, "For a long time, I've admired the compassionate style of practice in this place. Arriving here, I only see a coarse brute."

Chan Master Zhichang said, "The way you talk, are you coarse or am I?"

Still upset, the student monk asked, "What is coarse?"

Chan Master Zhichang put down the hoe.

The student monk then asked, "What is fine?"

The Chan Master raised the hoe and struck the pose of chopping the snake.

The student monk did not understand Chan Master Zhichang's meaning and said, "The 'coarse' and 'fine' you speak of, people are unable to understand."

Chan Master Zhichang asked in return, "For the time being, let's not speak of 'coarse' and 'fine' in this way. May I ask, where and when did you see me chop the snake?"

Not at all courteous, the student monk said, "Right here and now!"

Chan Master Zhichang admonished, "You, 'right here and now,' do not see yourself but come here to see the chopping of the snake—what are you doing?"

The student monk finally had an awakening.

In the history of the Chan School, there is the story of Chan Master Nanquan killing a cat.[1] Some say that no killing is a fundamental precept in Buddhism, and Nanquan should not kill. Some say that this was Nanquan's great capacity and great application, and we cannot use a narrow perspective to slander a great sage. Nanquan chopping the cat—perhaps he was striking the pose with his hands to cut off our material desire and attachment. In the case of Zhichang chopping the snake, this may have also been striking the pose of chopping. The student monk, seeing the wind, took it for rain. Therefore, without thinking, he criticized the Chan Master for being too coarse, implying that he had no compassion at all.

However, since Chan Master Zhichang had a virtuous reputation, he could draw in students. How could anyone be allowed to speak of "coarse" and "fine"? Therefore, he admonished the student monk not to linger in sight, sound, sensation, and perception. In Chan, we should cut off ordinary sentiment and knowledge. Why do we have to differentiate and attach to external phenomena, and why are we unable to take care of ourselves right here and now?

The Moon Cannot Be Stolen

When he was not propagating the Dharma, Zen Master Ryokan usually lived in a plain and crude thatched hut at the foot of a mountain. His life was very simple. One night, as he was returning from teaching the sutras, he bumped into a thief who was in his grass hut. When the thief saw that the Zen Master[2] had returned, he panicked, not knowing what to do.

Ryokan kindly said to the empty-handed thief, "Can't find anything to steal? I think you made this trip in vain. How about this? The clothes I'm wearing, just take them.

The thief snatched the clothes and fled. Zen Master Ryokan, standing naked in the moonlight, watched the retreating figure of the thief and sighed with infinite regret, "It's a pity I can't give him this beautiful moon!"

The "beautiful moon" symbolizes our intrinsic nature. In one's intrinsic nature, every person has an unlimited treasure. If we could recognize the treasure within us, why would we need to steal things from others? Zen Master Ryokan's regret over not being able to give others the beautiful moon tells the sentient beings of the world that everyone has the most precious treasure–our Buddha nature. Why should we degrade ourselves by becoming thieves?

吾有一躯佛也，人皆不识、不塑亦不装，不雕亦不刻，无一堆泥土、无一点彩色、工画画不出、贼偷偷不得，体相本自然、清净常皎洁、此是真身、何劳身分千百亿。

《月亮偷不去》

良宽题句如偷

Transcend the Ordinary and the Sacred

When Chan Master Nanta Guangyong first went to study with Chan Master Yangshan, Yangshan asked him, "What have you come here for?"

Guangyong answered, "I've come to pay my respects to the Chan Master."

Yangshan then asked, "Have you seen the Chan Master?"

Guangyong answered, "I've seen him."

Yangshan further asked, "Is the Chan Master's appearance like a donkey or a horse?"

Guangyong said, "I think the Chan Master is also not like a Buddha!"

Yangshan would not let up and proceeded to ask, "If he's not like a Buddha, then what is he like?"

Not wanting to be outdone, Guangyong answered, "If he's like anything at all, then what difference is there from a horse or donkey?"

Yangshan exclaimed in great admiration, "You've transcended the ordinary and the sacred! Emotions ceased, true essence revealed. In the next twenty years, no one will surpass you. Take good care of yourself."

After this, whenever Chan Master Yangshan met anyone, he would say in praise, "Guangyong is a Buddha in the flesh."

What, exactly, is the meaning contained within this gongan? For instance, some have asked, what are people like? This is a very difficult question to answer because if there are things they are like, then there are things they are not like. If we answer that people are like ghosts, then there are also people among ghosts. If we say ghosts are like people, then there are also ghosts among people. The Diamond Sutra *says, "All forms are illusory. If we see that the various forms are formless, then we see the Tathagata." What is space[3] like? Space is without form and without formlessness. Because space has no form, it can embrace the myriad phenomena. Space has no form, so it is like the forms of all phenomena. Chan Master Yangshan and Chan Master Guangyong debated that he was not like a donkey and not like a Buddha. Then what exactly was he like? He was like himself. Only by seeing our own intrinsic nature can we be as one with space. What is it like? It is like the form of space without form. If we are able to transcend the ordinary and the sacred, and if essence and function are one, then that is seeing the truth of formlessness.*

One and Ten

Chan Master Longtan Chongxin was a native of Hunan Province. Before becoming a monk, he was extremely poor. Next to Chan Master Tianhuang Daowu's temple, he set up a stand selling cakes. He did not even have a place to live. Chan Master Daowu took pity on his destitution, and gave him a small room in the temple to reside in. To show his gratitude, Chongxin sent ten cakes to Chan Master Daowu every day. After receiving them, Chan Master Daowu would always have his attendant take one to give back to Chongxin. One day, Chongxin finally protested to Chan Master Daowu, "The cakes are my gift to you. How can you return one to me each day? What is the meaning of this?"

Chan Master Tianhuang Daowu explained gently, "If you can give me ten every day, why can't I return one to you every day?"

Unconvinced, Chongxin countered, "Since I can give ten to you, why would I care to have you return one to me?"

Daowu roared with laughter and said, "Are you complaining that one is too few? If I haven't complained that ten is too many, how can you still complain that one is too few?"

After Chongxin heard this, he seemed to have an awakening. He then resolutely requested Chan Master Daowu to tonsure him and allow him to become a monk.

Chan Master Daowu said, "One gives rise to ten, ten gives rise to a hundred, and can even give rise to millions. All dharmas originate from one."

Chongxin confidently answered, "One gives rise to all dharmas; all dharmas are one."

Chan Master Daowu tonsured him. Afterwards, he settled in Longtan, building a small hut to live in. He came to be known as Chan Master Longtan Chongxin.

This gongan completely shows the oneness of self and other, and the Chan mind in which there is no duality between subject and object. Chan Master Tianhuang Daowu's house—by allowing Chan Master Longtan Chongxin to go live in it, this demonstrated that what is mine is yours. Chan Master Longtan Chongxin's cakes—after Chan Master Tianhuang Daowu accepted them and then returned one to Chan Master Longtan Chongxin, this demonstrated that what is yours is mine. Of course, at the time, the great pains taken by Chan Master Tianhuang Daowu could not be understood by an ordinary person who sold cakes. However, constantly interacting like this finally triggered Chongxin's epiphany. From contemplating this ball of doubt to directly debating, Longtan Chongxin ultimately awakened to the non-duality of many and few, the non-duality of you and me, the non-duality of mind and matter, and the non-duality of with and without. It turns out the myriad things in the universe, with their numerous differences, are all one Chan mind.

一生十生百生，宇宙萬有皆一禪心。

《一禪心》道悟於龍潭崇信

Not Changing Responds to Myriad Changes

Chan Master Daoshu built a temple by a Daoist[4] shrine. The Daoist priests could not stand this Buddhist temple near their shrine. Therefore, every day, they conjured a number of demons and ghosts to harass the monastics in the temple, wanting to frighten them away. Today, they would summon wind and invoke rain. Tomorrow, the wind would whip up and lightning would flash. This actually caused quite a few young novice monks to be scared away. However, Chan Master Daoshu lived there for more than ten years. Finally, the Daoist priests exhausted the tricks that they conjured up, but Chan Master Daoshu still would not leave. Without any choice, the Daoist priests could only give up their Daoist shrine and move elsewhere.

Afterwards, some people asked Chan Master Daoshu, "The Daoists are skilled in the magic arts! How were you able to prevail over them?"

The Chan Master replied, "I had nothing that could surpass them. But if I'm forced to speak, only with the word 'not' could I prevail over them."

"'Not?' How could that surpass them?"

The Chan Master said, "They have the magic arts. To 'have' is to have limits, to have an end, to have measurements, to have boundaries. Yet, I do not have the magic arts. 'Not' is not having limits, not having an end, not having measurements, and not having boundaries. The relationship between 'not' and 'have' is that no change[5] responds to myriad changes. My 'not changing' of course, prevails over their 'changing'."

Not Believing Is the Ultimate Truth

A student monk requested instruction from Imperial Master Huizhong: "The ancient sage said,

The verdant green bamboo all are Dharmakaya;
The luxuriant yellow flowers are nothing but prajna.

Non-believers think this wrong; believers think it is inconceivable. But I do not know what is correct?"

Imperial Master Huizhong replied, "Such is the state of beings like Manjusri Bodhisattva and Samantabhadra Bodhisattva. It is not something that ordinary people and Hinayana practitioners can believe or accept, so the *Flower Ornament Sutra* says, 'The Buddhakaya permeates all dharma realms, universally manifests before all beings, and following conditions, responds to seekers completely. Yet, it eternally dwells in this bodhi seat.' Since the green bamboo does not go beyond the dharma realms, what is not the Dharmakaya? In addition, the *Prajna Sutras* say, 'Form is limitless, thus, prajna is also limitless.' Since yellow flowers do not go beyond form, what is not prajna? Therefore, the sutras originally are undetermined Dharmas, and the Dharma originally is without many seeds."[6]

After the student monk listened to this, he still did not understand. He then asked, "As to that statement, are the believers correct? Are the non-believers correct?"

Imperial Master Huizhong, hinting at an even higher state of mind, answered, "The believers are the mundane truth; the non-believers are the ultimate truth."

Astonished, the student monk said, "The non-believers ridicule it as wrong view! How can the Chan Master say they are the ultimate truth?"

"The non-believers, themselves, do not believe the ultimate truth, itself, is the ultimate truth. Because it is the ultimate truth, ordinary people denounce it as wrong. Those with wrong views—how can they speak the ultimate truth?" Imperial Master Huizhong concluded.

Just then, the student monk awakened to the ultimate truth, which is not easy to believe.

When the Buddha first attained enlightenment, he lamented that what he had awakened to went against sentient beings' beliefs. Sentient beings think sensual pleasures are real; the Buddha realized sensual pleasures are false. Sentient beings think that Buddha nature and suchness do not exist; the Buddha held they do. As a result, in the ways of the mundane world, there is no one who does not use belief or non-belief as standards, there is no one who does not use speaking of good or bad as standards. The truth is that those on the Buddha Way belong to the Buddha Way, and those with wrong views belong to wrong views.

真俗二諦┊黃花無非般若翠竹悉是法身┊人不信是真諦

I'm Not a Sentient Being

Chan Master Weikuan was once asked by a student monk, "Do dogs have Buddha nature?"

"They do," answered Chan Master Weikuan.

"Do you have Buddha nature?"

"I don't."

"Why do all sentient beings have Buddha nature, yet you do not?"

"Because I am not the sentient being you are talking about."

"You're not a sentient being. Are you a Buddha?"

"I'm not that either."

"Then what exactly are you?"

"I'm not a 'what'!"

The student monk finally asked, "Then, is it something we can see or think of?"

"It is the inconceivable, beyond thinking and beyond discussing."

What am I? I am myself. If everyone could affirm the self, then that is the true self. That which we call the true "self" is neither sentient being nor non-sentient being. Then what is it?

鶴眼三星似君不須持世策功勲风和日暖黄鶴叫春在花枝已十分

《一赤不是衆生》 憨寬給學僧

Cannot Take Your Place

Chan Master Daoqian and his good friend, Zongyuan, traveled far and wide together to visit and study.[7] On the way, Zongyuan could not bear the fatigue of crossing mountains and rivers, so he grumbled time and again about wanting to turn back.

Daoqian comforted him, saying, "We already pledged to go forth to study, and we've also walked such a long way. Now, giving up halfway and going back would be a real shame. How about this: from now on, if there is anything I can do for you along the way, I will certainly do it for you. However, there are only five things I can't help you with."

Zongyuan asked, "What five things?"

Daoqian said very matter-of-factly, "Dress, eat, shit, piss, and walk."

With Daoqian's words, Zongyuan finally had a great awakening. From then on, he never again dared to speak of hardship.

As the saying goes: "When gold flows in with the tide, you should still get up early to scoop it up!" In this world, there is no achievement that can be attained without effort. A thousand-foot tower rises from the ground up; a journey of a thousand miles begins with a single step. In afflictions[8] and the cycle of birth and death, other people cannot take our place in the slightest. Everything depends on oneself!

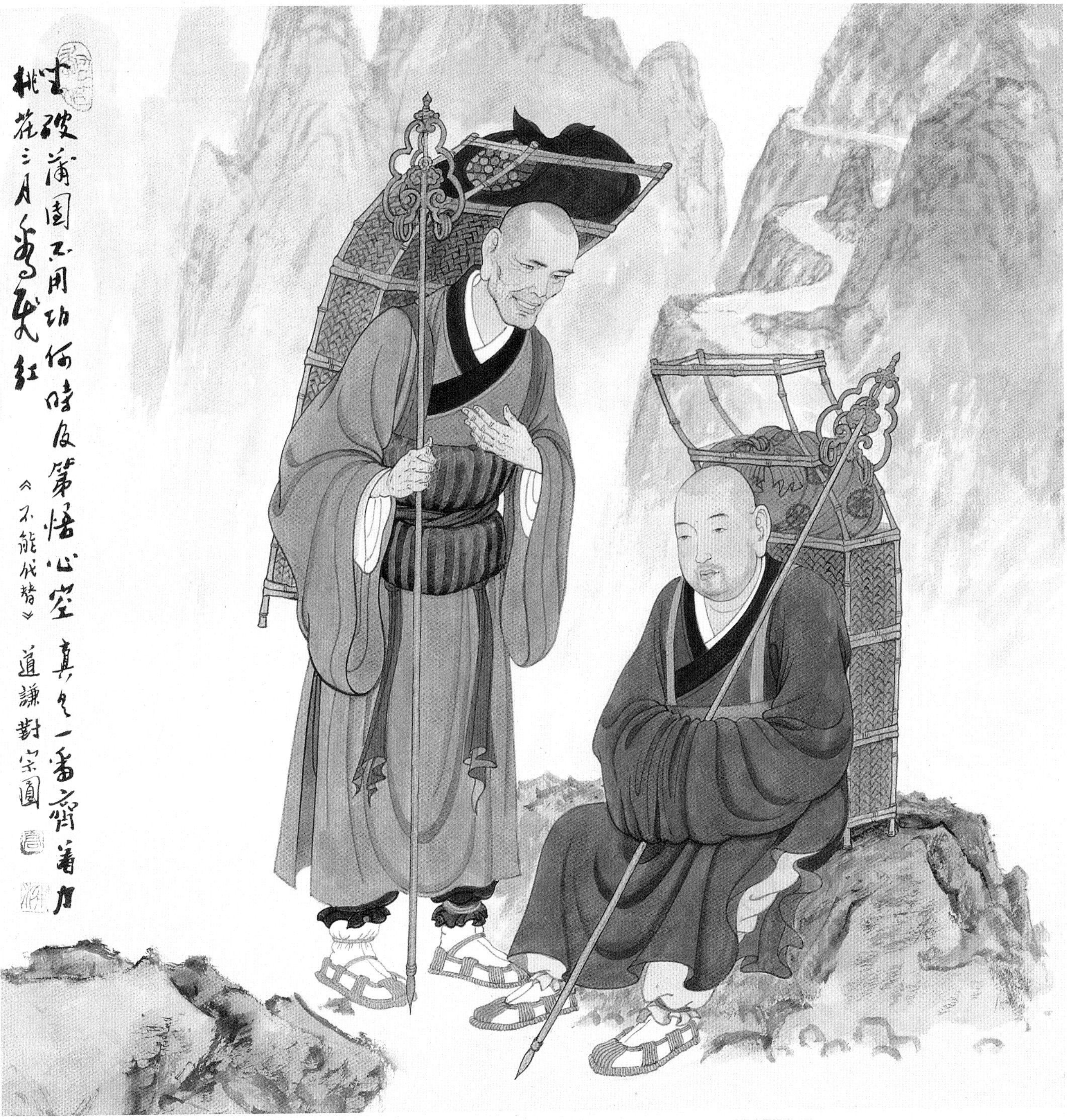
坐破蒲團不用功
何時及第悟心空
真正一番齊著力
桃花三月看飛紅
《不能代替》
道謙對宗圓

Let Go of What?

During the Buddha's lifetime, there was a Brahman named Heizhi[9] who came before the Buddha.

Using his supernatural powers, he held two vases in his hands and came forward to offer them to the Buddha.

The Buddha said to Brahman Heizhi, "Let go!"

The Brahman put down the vase he held in his left hand.

The Buddha again said, "Let go!"

The Brahman then put down the vase he held in his right hand.

But, the Buddha still said to him, "Let go!"

At this time, Brahman Heizhi said, "I'm already empty-handed. There's nothing else I can put down. May I ask what you want me to let go of now?"

The Buddha said, "I did not ask you to put down your vases. What I want you to let go of are your six sense organs, six dusts, and six consciousnesses. When you completely let go of them, without anything left, then you will liberated from the shackles of birth and death."

Only then did Brahman Heizhi understand the Buddha's teaching of "letting go."

"Let go!" This is very difficult to accomplish. Once we have power and fame, we cannot let go of power and fame. Once we have money, we cannot let go of money. Once we have love, we cannot let go of love. Once we have a career, we cannot let go of the career.

The heavy burdens on our shoulders and the stress in our minds are much more than the vases in our hands. We can say these heavy burdens and pressures make our lives very hard. When we need it, the Buddha's instruction to "let go" can be regarded as a path to happiness and liberation!

Arrive at Longtan

Chan Master Deshan was a great master who lectured on the sutras and the Dharma in the North. Because he was dissatisfied with the Southern Chan School's method of "special transmission outside the scriptures,"[10] carrying his work *The Blue Dragon Commentary on the Diamond Sutra*, he went to the South to debate. No sooner had he arrived in the South than he had to endure an old granny's taunting.[11] From then on, he reined in his overbearing ego. He also asked the old lady if there was a great master nearby whom he could visit and study with. The old lady told him that five *li*[12] away, there was a Chan Master Longtan who was very accomplished.

When Chan Master Deshan arrived at Longtan,[13] as soon as he saw Chan Master Longtan, he eagerly asked, "What is this place?"

Chan Master Longtan answered, "Longtan!"

Chan Master Deshan asked more insistently, "Since it is called Longtan, as I walk around here, I don't see dragons and I don't see ponds. Why is this?"

Chan Master Longtan directly told Chan Master Deshan, "You've gone to great lengths to get here. You have arrived at Longtan!"

That very night, Deshan went to seek instruction from Chan Master Longtan. He stood before the seated Chan Master Longtan for a long time, not leaving. Chan Master Longtan said, "It is very late. Why won't you go?"

Deshan bid him good night and took his leave. He got to the door, then came back and said, "It's really too dark outside. I'm new here and do not know my way around."

Chan Master Longtan lit a candle for him, but just as Deshan reached out to take it, Chan Master Longtan blew out the flame. At that moment, Deshan suddenly had a great awakening. He immediately knelt down and bowed to Chan Master Longtan.

Chan Master Longtan asked, "What did you see?"

Chan Master Deshan replied, "From this day forward, with regard to the tongues of all Chan Masters under Heaven,[14] I will never again have any doubts."

The next day, Chan Master Deshan took out his commentary and burned it. As the flames rose, he said, "Exhausting all abstruse debates is like sending a single hair into the universe; exhausting the matters of the world is like casting a single droplet into a great valley."

The sutras, no matter how profound the lectures, are still discriminating knowledge. The Chan School is without words–ultimately, it is the awakening of the non-differentiating mind. The night is dark; lighting a candle, then blowing it out signifies that after external light is extinguished, the Chan light of the inner mind will begin to glow. With this Chan light, we clearly see our true self. What we call language, the written word, and discriminating consciousness are all droplets in a great ocean.

I'm an Attendant

The Imperial Master Nanyang Huizhong was grateful for his attendant's thirty years of service and wanted to repay him by helping him attain awakening. One day, he called out, "Attendant!"

As soon as the attendant heard the Imperial Master call him, he immediately responded, "Imperial Master, what do you need?"

The Imperial Master said helplessly, "Nothing!"

After a while, the Imperial Master again called out, "Attendant!"

The attendant immediately replied, "Imperial Master, what do you need?"

Once again, the Imperial Master said helplessly, "Nothing!"

After many times of this, the Imperial Master changed his approach towards the attendant, crying out, "Buddha! Buddha!"

Completely at a loss, the attendant asked in return, "Imperial Master, whom are you calling?"

The Imperial Master had no choice but to instruct clearly, "I'm calling you!"

The attendant did not understand, so he said, "Imperial Master, I'm an attendant, not a Buddha!"

This time, Imperial Master Huizhong could only sigh with lament, "In the future, do not blame me for letting you down, when in fact, it is you who has let me down!"

The attendant still obstinately said, "Imperial Master! No matter what, I will never let you down and you will never let me down!"

The Imperial Master said, "The truth is, you've already let me down."

Imperial Master Huizhong and the attendant—who let whom down? Let us not discuss it. However, the attendant only recognized himself as an attendant and was afraid to shoulder the title of Buddha. This is extremely regrettable. The Chan School stresses, "directly shouldering responsibilities." What we call the mind, Buddha, and sentient being are no different. However, sentient beings only recognize themselves as sentient beings and do not recognize themselves as Buddhas. They sink in the cycle of birth and death, and are unable to return home. This is very sad!

Chan Master Wumen said,[15]

> *Wanting others to shoulder an iron cangue[16] without openings,*
> *Implicates the descendants, giving them no rest.*
> *Wanting to support the door and prop up the house,*
> *You must climb up a mountain of knives barefoot!*

The Imperial Master, advanced in years and of solitary mind, used the method of "pressing an ox's head down to eat the grass" on the attendant to make him awaken. It could not be helped that the attendant was only an attendant, not a Buddha.

The Manifestation of Manjusri

Chan Master Wenxi was on a pilgrimage to Mt. Wutai.[17] Before he arrived, he stayed overnight in a thatched hut where an old man lived. Wenxi asked the old man, "How is it in this place of practice?"

The old man replied, "Dragons and snakes intermix; the ordinary and the sacred intermingle."

Wenxi asked, "How many live here?"

The old man answered, "Three three in front, three three in back."[18]

When Wenxi woke up the next day, the thatched hut had disappeared, and he saw Manjusri riding a lion hovering in midair. He regretted that though he had eyes, he had not recognized the bodhisattva and let a chance slip by.

When Wenxi later went to study with Chan Master Yangshan, he attained awakening. Therefore, he settled down to work as a cook. One day, amidst the steam from the rice cooker he again saw the manifestation of Manjusri. Wenxi then raised a wooden rice spoon, struck, and said, "Manjusri is Manjusri; Wenxi is Wenxi. You won't fool me today!"

Manjusri recited a gatha:

> Bitter melons are bitter even at the root,
> Sweet melons are sweet to the stem;
> Cultivating over three great kalpas,
> Yet, snubbed[19] by this monk.

Because we do not understand our intrinsic nature, we seek the Dharma outside of our mind from morning to night. Therefore, we worry about gains and losses. If we could awaken to our intrinsic nature, then "Manjusri is Manjusri; Wenxi is Wenxi." Although the two are different, they are actually not different. Why should we be regretful or troubled then?

In Manjusri's gatha, he was not afraid of others snubbing him, but rather, was explaining that after three great kalpas of cultivation, only today did he truly come across a close friend, someone who really knew him.

All along, Manjusri and Wenxi were one and the same!

I'm Here

Chan Master Yunyan Tancheng and Chan Master Daowu Yuanzhi of Changsha were both disciples of Chan Master Yaoshan Weiyan, and they had a very close friendship. Chan Master Daowu, forty-six years of age when he became a monk, was eleven years older than Yunyan. One day, Chan Master Yunyan fell ill. Chan Master Daowu then asked him, "If you leave this leaking shell, where are you going and when can we see each other again?"

Without any hesitation, Chan Master Yunyan said, "The place without arising and without extinction."

Chan Master Daowu disagreed and offered a different view, "Why not say the place not without arising and without extinction, and also that we do not seek to see each other?"

After Chan Master Daowu said this, without waiting for Yunyan's reply, he picked up his bamboo hat and headed outside. Chan Master Yunyan then said, "Please wait a moment before you go. I want to ask you, what are you taking that hat for?"

Chan Master Daowu replied, "It has its uses."

Chan Master Yunyan asked more insistently, "When the wind and rain come, what is it for?"

Chan Master Daowu replied, "It's covered."[20]

Yunyan asked, "Is it still being covered or not?"

Daowu said, "Even though this is the case, it must also be without outflow."

When Yunyan had recovered from his illness, he was brewing tea because he was thirsty. Chan Master Daowu asked, "What are you doing?"

Yunyan said, "Making tea!"

Daowu asked, "Making tea for whom?"

Yunyan said, "Someone wants to drink it!"

Daowu asked, "Why doesn't he brew it himself?"

Yunyan said, "Fortunately, I'm here."

Yunyan and Daowu were Dharma brothers, but they had different styles of practice. Daowu was active and enthusiastic; Yunyan was old-fashioned and reserved. But, in terms of their cultivation, they were mutually encouraging and supportive, and they never bore grudges against one another. When they were discussing birth and death, one spoke of seeing each other in the place with arising and extinction and the other spoke of seeing each other in the place without arising and extinction. "Arising and extinction" and "without arising and extinction" are actually one and the same in the Chan practitioner's mind. Daowu took a bamboo hat to let his intrinsic nature be without outflow. A house and a teacup that leak are not good vessels. If we can attain the state without outflow (staying far away from affliction), then we become complete beings. While Yunyan was sick and discussing birth and death, he was very detached. When discussing the brewing of tea, his response was "Fortunately, I'm here." This kind of self-affirmation, not following birth and death, not differentiating between with and without, is the liberation of Chan.

肯定自我不隨生死不計有望即獲解脫

《有表画》雲晟與圓智

Help Yourself with Your Own Umbrella

A devotee was taking shelter from the rain under the eaves of a house. He saw a Chan master walking by holding an umbrella, so he called out, "Chan master! Help out a sentient being! How about taking me along for a short distance?"

The Chan master said, "I'm in the rain. You're under the eaves, and under the eaves, there's no rain. You don't need my help."

The devotee immediately walked out from under the eaves, stood in the rain, and said, "Now I'm also in the rain. You should help me!"

The Chan master replied, "I'm in the rain; you're also in the rain. I'm not drenched by the rain because I have an umbrella; you're soaked because you don't have an umbrella. Therefore, it's not me helping you but the umbrella helping me. If you want to be 'helped,' you needn't look to me. Please find yourself an umbrella!"

After saying this, he left!

With our own umbrella, we can avoid being drenched by the rain. With our own true Buddha nature, we should not be deluded by Mara. Not bringing an umbrella on a rainy day and wanting other people to help us is like not finding the true intrinsic nature in usual times and wanting others to liberate us. If we do not use our own treasure and only think about that of others, how can we be satisfied? Help ourselves with our own umbrella; liberate ourselves through our own intrinsic nature—in everything we must look to ourselves. The Chan master's unwillingness to lend his umbrella is the Chan master's great compassion.

時師度悟特自度

《自鋒自度》 禪師知信書

Mind and Nature

There was a student monk who went to Imperial Master Nanyang Huizhong's place to study. He asked for instruction, saying, "Chan is another name for mind, and 'mind' is the true nature of suchness that is neither increased in Buddhas nor decreased in the ordinary. The patriarchs of the Chan School changed the term 'mind' to 'nature.' May I ask the Chan Master, what is the difference between 'mind' and 'nature'?"

Huizhong replied without the slightest reservation, "When deluded, there is a difference; when awakened, there is no difference."

The student monk then, taking it a step further, asked, "The sutras say, 'Buddha nature is eternal; the mind is impermanent.' Why would you say that there's no difference?"

Imperial Master Huizhong patiently explained by way of analogy: "You're only relying on words, and not relying on the meaning. For example, when it's cold, water solidifies into ice; when it's warm, ice melts into water. When deluded, nature solidifies into mind; when awakened, mind melts into nature. Mind and nature are originally the same. Depending on delusion or awakening, there is a difference."

The student monk finally came to a deep understanding.

In Buddhism, there are many names for "mind" and "nature," such as: "the original face," "Tathagatagarbha," "Dharmakaya," "the ultimate truth," "intrinsic nature," "suchness," "the essence," "true mind," "prajna," "Chan," etc. This is nothing other than applying various ways for us to recognize ourselves. Although there is a difference between delusion and awakening, there is no difference in true nature. For example, gold is gold, yet it can be made into earrings, rings, bracelets, and various kinds of gold objects. Although these objects may be different, they are really all gold. Understand this: though the terms mind and nature are different, they both actually refer to our own essence.

迷时凭性
逞时缘红
暖时融液
以此移
迷时封性
为一时转以
成性

《心与性》
東陽華
示興手順

How Heavy

Su Dongpo, a scholar of the Hanlin Imperial Academy,[21] once had a discussion with Chan Master Zhaojue about the Way. After talking about "sentient and non-sentient beings both having the perfect wisdom of the Buddhas," he suddenly had an awakening. As a result, he composed three gathas entitled, "Before Practicing Chan," "While Practicing Chan," and "After Practicing Chan and Awakening to the Way" to show his attainments. The state before practicing Chan was:

> Viewed directly, a ridge; from the side, a peak,
> Far, near, high, and low are all unique;
> Not knowing the true face of Mt. Lu,[22]
> Only because one is on the mountain.

While practicing Chan, his state of mind was:

> Misty rains of Mt. Lu, tides of Zhejiang,
> Yet to arrive, thousands of regrets do not cease;
> Even when one returns, there isn't even a thing,
> Misty rains of Mt. Lu, tides of Zhejiang.

After practicing Chan and awakening to the Way, his state of mind was:

> The babbling creeks are the broad, long tongue;[23]
> The scenic mountains are nothing but the pure body.[24]
> Nightfall brings eighty-four thousand gathas,
> In days ahead, how to present them to others?

After this Chan awakening, Su Dongpo thought even more highly of his understanding of the Dharma. When he heard that Chan Master Chenghao of Yuquan Temple in Southern Jingzhou had an advanced Chan practice and that his sharp wit was difficult to reach, Su Dongpo was entirely unconvinced. Therefore, in civilian clothes, he sought an audience with the Chan Master, wanting to test Chan Master Chenghao's attainment. When they first met, Su Dongpo said, "I heard the Chan Master's attainment of Chan awakening is profound. May I ask, what is Chan awakening?"

Chan Master Chenghao did not answer and asked instead, "May I inquire after the honorable official's surname?"

Su Dongpo said, "My surname is Cheng,[25] the 'cheng' that weighs how heavy all the elders of the world are!"

Chan Master Chenghao shouted loudly and said, "Please tell me: how heavy is this shout?"

Su Dongpo had nothing to counter with, so he bowed and withdrew.

The three levels of Su Dongpo's Chan practice are exactly like the three stages of Chan practice described by Chan Master Qingyuan Xingsi. He said, "Before practicing Chan, we see mountain as mountain, we see water as water. While practicing Chan, we see mountain not as mountain, we see water not as water. After practicing Chan, we see mountain is still mountain, we see water is still water."

When Chan practitioners pass through these three critical junctures, even though they can awaken, it is by no means an attainment of cultivation. Awakening is understanding, and cultivation belongs to attainment. Therefore, Chan practitioners begin to cultivate from awakening, and through cultivation achieve attainment. If those without attainment of cultivation were to come across a great Chan teacher like Chan Master Chenghao, and he shouted at them, they would be rendered wide-eyed and tongue-tied.

High and Far

The student monks of the Chan Hall at Longhu Temple[26] were copying a painting of a fierce battle between a dragon and a tiger onto the enclosing wall in front of the monastery. In the painting, the dragon was circling amidst the clouds, about to swoop down, while the tiger crouched on a mountaintop, getting ready to pounce. Even though the monks had altered it many times, they still thought the dynamics in the painting were insufficient. Just by chance, Chan Master Wude was returning from outside, so the student monks asked the Chan Master to critique their work.

After Chan Master Wude looked it over, he said, "The outward appearance of the dragon and tiger were drawn quite well, but how much do you know about the characteristics of dragons and tigers? Now, what you should understand is that before a dragon attacks, it must draw back its head; when a tiger is going to pounce upward, it must lower its head. The greater the angle a dragon's neck is drawn back and the closer a tiger's head is to the ground, then the faster they can charge forward and the higher they can leap."

The student monks very happily received this advice and said, "Teacher, your words really cut to the point! We not only drew the dragon's head too far forward, but the tiger's head is also too high. No wonder we always felt that the dynamics were insufficient."

Chan Master Wude took the opportunity to instruct them, saying, "The principles of conducting oneself, handling affairs, practicing Chan, and cultivating the Way are also the same. Only after retreating a step to prepare, can one charge ahead even farther. Only after humble self-reflection can one climb even higher."

Seeming not to understand, the student monks asked, "Teacher, how can one who retreats move forward? How can a humble person go even higher?"

Chan Master Wude said earnestly, "Just listen to my Chan poem,

> Planting a field full of green seedlings by hand,
> Lowering my head, I then see the sky in the water.
> When body and mind are pure, this is the Way,
> Stepping back is, in fact, moving forward.

Do all of you comprehend the meaning?"

At that, the student monks were all able to understand.

Self-respect is one aspect of the Chan practitioner's character. They are sometimes independent and indomitable, proud and solitary, like a dragon raising its head and a tiger pouncing. But sometimes, they are very humble like a dragon drawing back and a tiger lowering its head. This explains that when we have to advance, advance; when we have to retreat, retreat; when we have to ascend, ascend; and when we have to descend, descend. This is what we call the grounds for advancing and retreating, and the timing for ascending and descending. The dragon is the spirit of beasts, the tiger the king of beasts. Chan practitioners are the virtuous among people, taking retreat as advance and modesty as esteem. Is this not fitting?

Nightly Wanderings

At the monastery where Zen Master Sengai lived, there was a student monk who often took advantage of nighttime, stealthily climbing over the monastery wall to go out and have some fun. Zen Master Sengai was making his rounds one night when he discovered a tall stool in the corner of the wall. Only then did it dawn on him that someone had been sneaking out. Without disturbing others, he simply moved the stool aside and stood in its place to wait for the student monk to return.

In the deep of night, the student monk returned from his wanderings. Unaware that the stool had been moved, he climbed over, stepped squarely on the head of Zen Master Sengai, and hopped to the ground. Only then did he clearly see that it was the Zen Master. He was so frightened he did not know what to do!

However, Zen Master Sengai, not minding in the least, comforted him, saying, "The night is deep and heavy with dew. Take care of your health: do not catch cold! Hurry back and put on some more clothes."

No one else in the entire monastery knew of this incident and Zen Master Sengai never mentioned it. However, from then on, not one of the monastery's more than one hundred student monks ever wandered out at night again.

The best education is an education of love. Using encouragement instead of reproach and consideration instead of punishment, it is even easier to receive the benefits of education.

Those like Zen Master Sengai take the unique characteristics of Chan education and develop them to the fullest. Chan education takes compassion and skillful means as its principles. Whether through blows and shouts, or strict discipline, we must first consider the student's capacity[27] before we can implement great compassion and skillful means. Parents and teachers everywhere should first consider the capabilities[28] of their children and students, and then apply the corresponding kind of education. Reform, loving-kindness, and personal example are the best Chan teachings.

禅門之教育
以慈悲為本
母以方便
為之行
不言身教

《在逝》

仙崖和尚書

I Can Be Busy for You Too

One time, Chan Master Foguang saw the Chan Monk Keqi and asked, "Since you came here to study Chan, time seems to have flown by. It's already been twelve autumns and winters.[29] Why have you never asked me about the Way?"

Chan Monk Keqi answered, "The elder Chan Master is very busy every day. I really do not dare to bother you!"

Time sped by, and another three years passed. One day, on the road, Chan Master Foguang ran into Chan Monk Keqi again and asked, "Do you have any questions about practicing Chan and cultivating the Way? Why haven't you come to ask me?"

Chan Monk Keqi replied, "The elder Chan Master is very busy. I dare not speak to you at will!"

Another year went by. When Chan Monk Keqi passed by Chan Master Foguang's room, the Chan Master again said to Keqi, "Come here. I have time today. Please come to my room to talk about the Way of Chan."

Chan Monk Keqi quickly joined palms and bowed, saying, "The elder Chan Master is very busy. How would I dare waste your time whenever I please?"

Chan Master Foguang knew that Chan Monk Keqi was too modest and would not have the courage to directly take responsibility. No matter how he practiced Chan, he would still not be able to awaken.

Chan Master Foguang knew he had to take the initiative, so when he ran into Chan Monk Keqi once again, he asked, "Learning the Way and practicing meditation require continuous investigation and contemplation. Why don't you ever come to ask me?"

Chan Monk Keqi still said, "Elder Chan Master, you are very busy. It is inappropriate for me to disturb you!"

Chan Master Foguang immediately shouted, "Busy! Busy! Busy for whom? I can be busy for you too!"

Chan Master Foguang's one statement, "I can be busy for you too!" struck a chord in Chan Monk Keqi's heart, and with these words, he immediately had an awakening.

Some people care too much about themselves and do not care about others. Even over little things, they bother others time and again. Some people care too much about others and are unwilling to act on their own behalf, ultimately losing many opportunities. The original face of Chan is to directly take responsibility. When it is time to eat, eat; when it is time to cultivate the Way, cultivate the Way; when it is time to ask questions, ask important questions; when it is time to answer, answer with certainty. Do not run around in circles, where what seems right is actually wrong!

I can help. Why do you not want me to help? You want me to help. Why can't I be busy for you too? Other and self—do not distinguish so clearly between them!

名醫化導有禾因
疾病傷寒先忌瞋
脈理深微能半性
良方精細度迷津

「我也可以渴飲羅漢，佛也就神奇頹疲。」

Antique Mirror Not Polished

When Chan Master Youdao first began his travels to study Chan, he passed by a teahouse. Because he was thirsty, he was on his way in to have a cup of tea and rest a while. As soon as the shopkeeper saw that it was a wandering monk, he greeted Youdao warmly and asked, "Chan Master, you must be tired! Want some tea?"

Chan Master Youdao casually glanced at the tea shelves and nodded his head, without saying any other words.

The shopkeeper seemed to also be a skilled Chan practitioner. He cautiously asked, "Presumably, you are a Chan master with a deeply profound practice. Chan Master, your humble servant would like to ask you a question. If you answer me, I will make an offering to you! How about it?"

Chan Master Youdao said, "Ask away!"

The shopkeeper asked, "When an antique mirror is not polished, how is it?"

Chan Master Youdao quickly answered, "It's pitch black."

The shopkeeper then asked, "After an antique mirror has already been polished, how is it?"

Chan Master Youdao replied, "It illuminates heaven and earth."

The shopkeeper took exception to this and said, "I'm sorry! Forgive me for not making an offering to you." So saying, he turned around and went back into the shop.

Chan Master Youdao was stunned. He thought, "I have practiced Chan for several decades, and now I don't even measure up to a shopkeeper! It is clear that his Chan practice is great." Subsequently, he resolved to take painstaking efforts to retreat into deep practice in search of awakening.

Three years later, Chan Master Youdao appeared once more at the doorway of the teahouse. Yet again, the shopkeeper greeted him kindly, "Ha! I haven't seen you for three years! But I still want to ask you that same old question: 'When an antique mirror is not polished, how is it?'"

Without a second thought, Chan Master Youdao said, "It's not far from here to Hanyang."[30]

The shopkeeper then asked, "After an antique mirror has already been polished, how is it?"

Chan Master Youdao answered, "Yingwu Islet is in front of Huanghe Pavilion."[31]

After the shopkeeper heard this, he sincerely said, "Chan Master, please accept my offering!" Immediately, he turned around and cried out, "Attendant! Make tea! Make tea! Make good tea!"

Was the antique mirror polished or not? Chan Master Youdao said that when it is not polished, it is pitch black; and when it is already polished, it illuminates heaven and earth. This antique mirror analogizes our intrinsic nature. Intrinsic nature is originally pure, without arising or ceasing, and shines brightly on its own. How is it possible to differentiate between not polished and already polished? Intrinsic nature does not increase in the sacred, nor does it decrease in the ordinary. Therefore, when Chan Master Youdao could not recognize the intrinsic nature that is like the antique mirror, it is no wonder he could not get any tea. The second time, he answered that when an antique mirror is not polished, "It's not far from here to Hanyang," and when an antique mirror is already polished, "Yingwu Islet is in front of Huanghe Pavilion." This showed that he could recognize the intrinsic nature was right here and now. So, he had good tea to drink.

多年古鏡要磨功
垢盡塵消始以融
掙脫枝杈亂念裡
亂心全消靜慮中

How Was It Ever Confused?

When he was traveling and studying, a wandering monk passed by a nunnery that an old lady took care of and stopped in front to rest. He asked the old woman, "Shigu,[32] in this nunnery, are there any other family members besides you?"

The old lady said, "Yes!"

The wandering monk asked, "Why don't I see them?"

The old lady replied, "Oh! The mountains, rivers, earth, grasses, and trees all are my family!"

The wandering monk then said, "Non-sentient beings are not sentient beings. How could these mountains, rivers, grasses, and trees ever have had the Shigu's appearance?"

The old lady replied, "Then, what do you think I look like?"

The wandering monk said, "An ordinary person!"

The old lady retorted, "You're also not a monastic!"

The wandering monk said, "Shigu! You mustn't confuse the Dharma."

The old lady replied, "I have not confused the Dharma at all!"

The wandering monk said, "An ordinary person in charge of a nunnery, becoming Dharma friends with grasses and trees. If this isn't confusing the Dharma, then what is it?"

The old lady responded, "Venerable, you can't say that. You should know you are a man and I am a woman. How was it ever confused?"

The myriad things of the universe are originally of one body—mind, Buddha, and sentient beings are without differentiation. However, we obstinately insist on separating this one body, this non-differentiation, and treating them with a differentiating mind. Therefore, in the mundane world, there are the different classifications of right and wrong, good and evil, sentient and non-sentient, and even male and female. When the myriad phenomena of the world appear, we treat them in this way endlessly. When speaking in terms of the dharma realm of suchness, then as in the old lady's case, how was it ever confused?

舍内分明有個人　無端答應山僧人　如門借宿非他也　你我原來都是人

《巖窟混清》書與僧弘老婆婆

Dadian and Han Yu

Emperor Xianzong of the Tang Dynasty[33] deeply venerated the Dharma, so he welcomed the relics of the Buddha into his palace to make offerings to the Buddha. One night, a bright light emanated from the palace. At the morning audience with the emperor, all of the officials offered their felicitations to the emperor. Only Han Yu did not. Moreover, he presented, "A Memorial on the Buddha's Bones," which denounced the Buddha as a barbarian. This infuriated the emperor who had a sincere faith in Buddhism. Therefore, he was demoted and sent to Chaozhou to serve as a provincial governor.

At that time, Chaozhou was located in the wild region of the South and the culture had not yet developed. Chan Master Dadian, whose cultivation was extraordinary, was held in high esteem by the people. Han Yu had heard that this region had a great monk. One day, with the intention of asking a difficult question, he went to pay Chan Master Dadian a visit. At that moment, the Chan Master had just entered samadhi while in sitting meditation. It was not a good time to come forward and ask questions. Therefore, he waited for a very long time. The attendant could see Han Yu's impatience, so he stepped forward and struck the signal hand bell three times by the Chan Master's ear. He whispered to the Chan Master, "First use samadhi to move, later use wisdom to eradicate."

The attendant's meaning was to say that the Chan Master's samadhi had already moved Han Yu's arrogant heart; now, to use wisdom to eradicate his attachments. After Han Yu, who was nearby, heard the attendant's words, he immediately bowed and withdrew. He said, "Fortunately, I have received this message from the attendant monk."

This time Han Yu did not ask for instruction. After a short period of time, Han Yu still felt that he could not untangle the knot of doubt in his mind. He paid another visit to Chan Master Dadian and asked, "May I inquire, Venerable, how many springs and autumns have you seen?"

Picking up his prayer beads, the Chan Master replied, "Understand?"

Unable to untangle the meaning, Han Yu said, "I don't!"

"Day and night, one hundred and eight."[34]

Han Yu still did not understand the meaning contained therein. The next day, he went again to seek instruction. Just as he walked up to the front gate, he saw a young novice monk. He went forward and asked, "How many springs and autumns has the Master seen?" The young novice monk remained silent and did not answer. Instead, he clicked his teeth three times. Han Yu felt like he had fallen into a dense fog. Once more, he went in to have an audience with Chan Master Dadian and ask for instruction. The Chan Master also clicked his teeth three times. Only then did Han Yu, as though he had awakened, say, "Oh, so the Dharma does not have two kinds. It is all the same."

What is the meaning of this gongan? Han Yu asked, "How many springs and autumns have you seen?" It was based on his knowledge and experience, and he wanted to make a great calculation with regard to time. In fact, time turns in unending cycles, without beginning and without end. So, how can we talk about its length? In unlimited time and space, life transmigrates[35] continuously. Clicking the teeth three times indicates that in endless life, we should not just show off our verbal skills. Aside from spoken and written words, we ought to truly experience and realize the Dharma, recognize our unlimited life, see our original face, and seek the eternal existence in the trichiliocosm.

學禪成佛
心中病
磨磚作境
眼中眼
一破牢關
笙鎮斷
尋閒信牛
便歸

《大顛心結癒》
大顛禪師悟

Extinguish the Fire in One's Mind

There was a general who had spent many years fighting on the battlefield and had grown tired of war. He made a special trip to see Chan Master Dahui Zonggao to request to become a monk. He said to Zonggao, "Chan Master, I have already seen through this world. Please Chan Master, compassionately take me in to become a monk. Let me be your disciple!"

Zonggao said, "You have a family and you have very strong secular habits. You still cannot become a monk. Give it some time and we'll talk about it later."

The general replied, "Chan Master! I can let go of everything now. My wife, my children, my family are all not a problem. Please tonsure me immediately."

Zonggao responded, "Give it some time and we'll talk about it later."

The general could do nothing.

One day, he rose very early and went to the temple to pay homage to the Buddha. Chan Master Dahui Zonggao said as soon as he saw him, "General, why have you come here so early to pay respect to the Buddha?"

The general, who was learning how to use Chan gathas, said,

> In order to extinguish the fire in the mind,
> Get up early to pay homage to the Buddhas.

The Chan Master jokingly also used a gatha to respond:

> Getting up so early in the morning,
> Not afraid your wife is being unfaithful?

Hearing this, the general became extremely angry and cursed, "You old monster! Your words are too hurtful!"

Chan Master Dahui Zonggao laughed heartily and said,

> With just a gentle fanning,
> The fire of your nature again burns.
> Such an irascible temperament,
> How can this be considered letting go?

Let go! Let go! Just because you say you have let go does not mean you are able to let go: "When talking, it seems like we are enlightened; when facing conditions, delusions arise." Likewise, habits are not changed just because we say we are able change them: "The rivers and mountains are easy to change; habitual tendencies[36] are difficult to get rid of." May I advise those who wish to study the Way and become monastics: Do not, because of a moment of impulse, become the laughingstock of others.

A Model through the Ages

After Chan Master Baizhang Huaihai of the Tang Dynasty succeeded Chan Master Mazu Daoyi, who founded the Chinese monastic community,[37] he drew up a set of systematic monastic rules–*The Monastic Regulations of Baizhang*.[38] This is what is known as "Mazu founded the Chinese monastic community, Baizhang established the monastic regulations." Chan Master Baizhang advocated the agricultural Chan lifestyle of "a day without working, a day without eating." He had already encountered many difficulties because Buddhism had up to that time taken precepts as the standard for life, but Chan Master Baizhang changed the system to take agricultural Chan as a lifestyle. There were even people who criticized him as a heretic.

Since the monastic community of which he was the abbot was on the peak of Mt. Baizhang, he was also called Chan Master Baizhang. Every day, besides leading the sangha in practice, he would always do the hard labor himself and work diligently. He was very earnest about the lifestyle of living by one's own efforts. With regard to trivial matters, he was especially unwilling to make others do the work for him.

Gradually, Chan Master Baizhang got older. Yet every day, he still went with his disciples up the mountain to carry firewood and down into the fields to farm because the agricultural Chan lifestyle is you grow what you eat. His disciples finally could not bear to let the old master do such hard physical labor, so the sangha community implored him not to follow the disciples out to work. However, Chan Master Baizhang still firmly said, "I am not virtuous enough to bother other people. Living in this world, if we don't do the work ourselves, wouldn't we become useless people?"

The disciples were unable to prevent the determined Chan Master from serving. All they could do was hide the Chan Master's carrying pole, his hoe, and other tools in order to keep him from working.

Chan Master Baizhang could do nothing but use not eating as a means of protest. His disciples anxiously asked why he was not drinking or eating.

Chan Master Baizhang said, "Since I don't work, how can I eat?"

The disciples had no choice but to return his tools to him and allow him to live as the sangha members did. The spirit of Chan Master Baizhang's "a day without working, a day without eating" has become a model for the monastic community through the ages.

Some people think that to contemplate Chan, you not only have to cut off worldly conditions completely, but that you also do not need to work. They think that they only have to do sitting meditation. In fact, if we do not work and we depart from life–where is there still Chan? To cure the sickness of Chan practitioners of the time, Chan Master Baizhang not only undertook the life of "a day without working, a day without eating," he even shouted out the slogan, "Chopping wood and carrying water is none other than Chan."

Whether reciting the Buddha's name or contemplating Chan, practice is not an excuse for laziness. I hope that the Chan practitioners of this generation will listen to what Chan Master Baizhang said.

Hundred Years, One Dream

Chan Master Jinshan Tanying was a native of Zhejiang Province. His surname was Qiu and his given name was Daguan. At the age of thirteen, he went to Longxing Temple and became a monk. When he was eighteen, he traveled to the capital and lived in Commanding General Li Duanyuan's garden. One day, the Commanding General asked him, "May I inquire Chan Master, the hell that people often talk about, does it actually exist or not?"

Chan Master Tanying answered, "When the Buddhas and Tathagatas spoke the Dharma, they spoke of existence from non-existence, like eyes seeing flowers in the sky. Does it exist or not? General, right now, you are in existence seeking non-existence. This is like trying to hold river water in your hands. While in this non-existence, manifesting existence is indeed laughable. If people see a prison before their eyes, why don't they see heaven in the mind? Joy and fear are in the mind, heaven and hell are just in a thought, and good and bad can both create conditions. General, just understand your mind and you will naturally have no delusion."

The Commanding General asked, "How is the mind realized?"

Tanying replied, "Don't think about good or evil."

The Commanding General then asked, "After not thinking, to where does the mind return?"

Tanying answered, "The mind returns nowhere. As the *Diamond Sutra* states, 'It should not abide, and then the mind will give rise.'"

The Commanding General asked, "When people die, where do they return to?"

Tanying said, "Not yet understanding life, how can you understand death?"

The Commanding General replied, "Regarding birth and life, I already understood."

Tanying said, "Please say a word about where life comes from."

At the moment the Commanding General was pondering this, Chan Master Tanying used his hands and pounded the General in the chest, saying, "What are you thinking here?"

The Commanding General answered, "I understand. I have only known to crave the journey of life, and was not aware I was wasting time."

Tanying said, "Hundred years, one dream."

Commanding General Li Duanyuan immediately awakened and recited a gatha, saying:

> Thirty-eight years,
> Ignorant and in a haze.
> Even if I have understanding,
> How is it different from ignorance?
> The Bian River flows smoothly,
> Its unchanging embankments are obscure.
> The army is returning,
> The arrow-like waves rush eastward.

Where does life come from? Where does death go? These are questions that the average person often thinks about; quite a few people even investigate these questions. However, no one breaks through this mystery. Sakyamuni Buddha and the Chan masters through the ages have presented the whole picture, one that is also not easily understood by people. Life has the ignorance[39] of being separate from one life to the next. The meaning is precisely that we change bodies and then do not know anything from the past. Therefore, from ancient times with regard to the "origin of life," many people have had widely diverse views with no agreement among them. In fact, the forms and appearances of life are myriad, but the principle of life is that everything is equal. When the meanings and principles of Buddhist dependent origination, emptiness, the Three Dharma Seals, karma, cause and effect, etc., are thoroughly understood, then questions like, "where life comes from" or "where death goes" can be known without asking.

Space Winks

One time at a Dharma function, Emperor Suzong of the Tang Dynasty sought instruction from Imperial Master Nanyang Huizhong, asking him many questions. However, the Chan Master did not even give him a glance. Emperor Suzong very angrily said, "I am the Son of Heaven of the Great Tang! How dare you not look at me?"

Without directly responding, Imperial Master Huizhong instead asked Emperor Suzong of the Tang Dynasty, "Oh, great emperor, have you ever seen space?"

"I've seen it!"

"Then, let me ask, has space ever winked at you?"

Emperor Suzong could say nothing in response.

In our lives, what we care about most are interpersonal relationships. Who is nice to me? Who treats me badly? Every day, we worry about gains and losses. If we are not haggling over money, then we are worrying about love. Besides these concerns about money and love, there are also the concerns about being respected. Throughout the day, we want people to praise us, we want people to hold us in high esteem, and we want people to notice us. Contrast this with space. Space does not need us to wink at it. Why would we need space to wink at us? The true principle of the Dharmakaya is like space. It vertically penetrates the three time periods; horizontally permeates the ten directions; fills the universe; and includes heaven and earth. According to conditions, it proceeds and responds. There is no place it is not. Emperor Suzong did not understand this. No wonder Imperial Master Nanyang asked, "Has space ever winked at you?"

Aspects of Life

At the first light of dawn, a layperson named Zhu Youfeng was cheerfully carrying a bouquet of fresh flowers and an offering of fruit. He was hurrying to take part in the morning chanting at Dafo Temple. Who would have guessed that just as he was stepping into the main shrine, a person would suddenly run out from the left and bump into Zhu Youfeng exactly at that moment, causing all the fruit he was holding to fall to the ground. Seeing the fruit all over the ground, Zhu Youfeng could not stand it and yelled, "Look! You're so careless. You've knocked over all of the fruit that I was going to offer to the Buddhas. How are you going to repay me?"

This person, named Li Nanshan, was very displeased and said, "What is knocked over is already knocked over. At most, saying 'I'm sorry' should be enough. Why do you need to be so ferocious?"

Zhu Youfeng was very angry and replied, "What kind of attitude is that? You are in the wrong, yet you blame others!"

It continued with them cursing each other. The noise of their mutual recriminations rose incessantly.

Chan Master Guangyu happened to pass by at this time. He took both of them aside and asked them exactly what had transpired. He then instructed them, saying, "You shouldn't walk in a careless manner. However, being unwilling to accept another person's apology is also wrong. Both of your behaviors were very foolish. Being able to honestly recognize our mistakes and to accept other people's apologies is, in fact, the behavior of the wise." After Chan Master Guangyu spoke, he continued, saying, "Living in this world, we have too many aspects of life that we must harmonize. For example, in society, how do we maintain harmony with our relatives and our friends? In education, how do we communicate with our teachers? With regard to personal finance, how do we regulate our expenses according to our incomes? With regard to family, how do we nurture the love between husband, wife, and children? In terms of health, how do we keep the body healthy? Spiritually, how do we select a lifestyle for ourselves? When we are able to do this, only then will we not fail to live up to our precious life. Think about this: over a little thing, you ruin a devout state of mind so early in the morning. Is it worth it?"

Li Nanshan spoke first, "Chan Master, I was wrong. I was really reckless." As he was speaking, he turned towards Zhu Youfeng and said, "Please accept my most sincere apologies. I was too foolish!"

Also from the bottom of his heart, Zhu Youfeng said, "I, too, was wrong. I shouldn't have lost my temper over such a small thing. It was very childish!"

The words of Chan Master Guangyu ultimately moved these two people who liked to fight and compete. Chan has high notes and also low notes.

No Merit at All

Emperor Wu of the Liang Dynasty[40] was a model ruler in Chinese history who supported Buddhism. When he was on the throne, he built numerous temples and erected a large number of Buddhist statues. He repaired and constructed bridges and roads for the welfare of the people. At that time, Chan Master Bodhidharma came from India to China to propagate the Dharma. Emperor Wu of Liang invited the Chan Master and asked him about the Dharma, saying, "In the way that I have continually done good deeds, what merit will I gain?"

"No merit at all," said Chan Master Bodhidharma, as though pouring a bucket of cold water on him.

Emperor Wu was very unhappy to hear this, and then asked him why. The Chan Master did not reply. In the end, because there was no meeting of the minds, he left with a flip of his sleeve.

In fact, how could Emperor Wu's good deeds have no merit at all? "No merit at all," which the Chan Master spoke of, explains the Chan Master's state of mind. The concept of duality between existence and non-existence in phenomena was not present. We just need to transcend our deluded attachment to this duality between existence and non-existence. Only then can we see through the reality of all dharmas, which is "there is non-existence, there is existence; there is not non-existence, there is not existence; there may be existence, there may be non-existence; there is originally existence, there is originally non-existence." This kind of transcendence is the path that every Chan practitioner must take. This kind of state is the original face of the Chan practitioner.

乳语帝武梁东摩达德功無今據根也昌来本禅乃果本典之有至其而有是非是有足無

The Imperial Master and the Emperor

One day, Emperor Shunzhi of the Qing Dynasty[41] invited Imperial Master Yulin to the palace, asking for instruction in the Dharma. Shunzhi asked, "In the *Surangama Sutra*, there is the so-called 'search for the mind in the seven locations,' asking where the mind is. Now, may I inquire, is the mind in the seven locations or not?"

Imperial Master Yulin replied, "Seeking the mind is impossible?"

Emperor Shunzhi then said, "The person who has awakened to the Way, does he still have joy, anger, sorrow, and happiness, or not?"

Imperial Master Yulin responded, "What is joy, anger, sorrow, and happiness?"

Emperor Shunzhi said, "The mountains, rivers, and this great earth arise from deluded thoughts. If deluded thoughts cease, then do the mountains, rivers, and this great earth still exist or not?"

Imperial Master Yulin said, "Like a person waking from a dream, do the things in the dream exist or not?"

Emperor Shunzhi then said, "How do I practice this?"

Imperial Master Yulin replied, "Act righteously, and let things take their course."

Emperor Shunzhi asked, "What is great?"

Imperial Master Yulin replied, "The light spreads in four directions and reaches above and below."

Emperor Shunzhi said, "How do I contemplate the original face?"

Imperial Master Yulin replied, "As the Sixth Patriarch said, 'Don't think of good, don't think of evil. At that moment, what is the original face?'"

Afterwards, whenever Emperor Shunzhi met people, he would say, "Having a conversation with Imperial Master Yulin really makes me regret meeting him so late."

Shunzhi was an emperor whose capacity for the Dharma was great. From his poem, "In Praise of the Sangha," we can know that his thinking was very much in accordance with the Dharma.

Before I was born, who was I?
When I was born, who was I?
When I grew into an adult, that is I;
When I close my eyes, who am I?
Not as good as not coming and not going,
Happy when coming, sad when going.
Sorrow, joy, separation, and reunion, many worries,
Who knows when I will be at ease?

Emperor Shunzhi was the ruler of a country, yet he envied the life of a monastic. He said,

Gold and jade are not precious,
Only wearing the kasaya over the shoulder is difficult;
One hundred years, thirty-six thousand days,
Is not as good as a half a day of a monk's ease.
The purple kasaya[42] exchanged for the yellow imperial robe
Only because that year's one erroneous thought;
Originally, I was to be a monk in the West,[43]
Why was I born in this Imperial House?

One could well imagine his respect for Imperial Master Yulin.
Imperial Master Yulin was an eminent monk of dignified bearing. Usually, he preferred silence and did not like to talk. Even when the emperor asked him about the Dharma, he was terse and to the point. Unwilling to say too much, he made people feel that a word of the Chan gate is not easy to seek.

時如何是本來面目
不思善不思惡正恁麼

國師告皇帝曰玉琳示順治

Originally Empty without Existence

One day, Chan Master Foyin ascended the high seat to give a discourse on the Dharma. Su Dongpo heard about this and hurried to attend. All the seats had already been taken; there were no empty places. The Chan Master, upon seeing Su Dongpo, said, "People have already filled the seats. This place has no seat for you, Scholar."

Su Dongpo, who had always been fond of Chan, immediately responded to the Chan Master, saying, "Since there are no seats, I will use the Chan Master's body of the four great elements and five aggregates as a seat."

Seeing that Su Dongpo wanted to debate Chan with him, the Chan Master then said, "Scholar! I have a question to ask you. If you can answer it, then this old monk's body can be taken as your seat. If you cannot answer it, then you have to leave the jade belt you are wearing at this temple as a memento." Su Dongpo had always thought highly of himself. He had no doubt that he would win, so he agreed. Chan Master Foyin then said, "The four great elements are originally empty and the five aggregates have no substantial existence. May I ask, Scholar, where do you want to sit?"

Su Dongpo was unable to utter a word.

Because our physical bodies are a temporary composition of the four great elements of earth, water, fire, and wind, they all do not have any real existence. Unable to peacefully sit here, Su Dongpo's jade belt was lost to Chan Master Foyin. It remains at Jinshan Temple to this very day.

What Are Lice Made Of?

One day, Su Dongpo and Qin Shaoyou were having a meal together. Because both of these men were very talented, they were often mutually unyielding on account of discussing and debating the Way. On this day, when they were eating, they just so happened to see a person walk by. Since he had not bathed for many days, his body was crawling with lice. Su Dongpo then said, "That person is really dirty. The filth on his body has given birth to the lice!" Qin Shaoyou, insisting on another opinion, said, "That's not so! The lice grew from the cotton batting in his clothes!" The two people each held fast to their opinions, arguing on with no resolution. They then decided to go ask Chan Master Foyin to make an impartial judgment, regarding how lice came about. Moreover, they mutually agreed that the person who lost the debate would have to give a banquet.

Striving to gain victory, Su Dongpo secretly ran to Chan Master Foyin's place and asked the Chan Master to help him by all means. After a while, Qin Shaoyou also went to ask for the Chan Master's help. Chan Master Foyin promised them. Both people thought for sure, they would be victorious. Feeling assured, they waited for the result of the judgment. The Chan Master decided, saying, "The head of the louse is born from the filth, but the feet of the louse grows from the cotton batting."

The Chan Master was a fine peacemaker. There was a poem that said,

A tree in the spring breeze has two conditions,
Southern branches face the warmth, northern ones face the chill.
Before me, a message coming from the West:[44]
One piece flies west, one piece flies east.

What does this poem tell us? It is the unity of things and self; things and self are one. The external forms of mountains, rivers, and this great earth are the internal mountains, rivers, and great earth. The great chiliocosm is precisely our internal world. Things and self already have no differentiation, and they are completely harmonized together. Just like on a tree, although they receive the same air, sunlight, and water, tree leaves actually have a different vitality. Moreover, they are able to not obstruct each other and exist on the same tree.

一樹春風有兩般南枝向暖北枝寒
瑶前一度西來意一片西來一片東

Can't Be Snatched Away

One day, Chan Master Linji followed his teacher, Chan Master Huangbo, down to the fields to work. Chan Master Linji walked behind Chan Master Huangbo. Chan Master Huangbo looked back and discovered Chan Master Linji's hands were empty and then said to him, "How come you forgot to bring your hoe?"

Chan Master Linji replied, "I don't know who took it."

Chan Master Huangbo stopped walking and said, "Come over here. I have something to discuss with you."

Chan Master Linji came forward. Chan Master Huangbo then stood his hoe upright, saying, "Only 'this.' There is no one in the world who can move it."

As soon as he heard those words, Chan Master Linji, rudely and immediately snatched the hoe from Chan Master Huangbo's hand. Firmly grasping it in his hand, he said, "Just a moment ago teacher, you said no one could move 'this.' Now, why is 'this' in my hand?"

Chan Master Huangbo said, "What is in the hand is not really in the hand, and what is not in the hand is not really not in the hand. Tell me, who will cultivate the fields for us today?"

Chan Master Linji replied, "Those who cultivate the field, let them cultivate. Those who harvest the field, let them harvest. What does this have to do with us?"

After Chan Master Linji said this, Chan Master Huangbo did not say a single word. He turned around and went back to the monastery.

Not long after, Chan Master Guishan asked Chan Master Yangshan about this matter, saying, "The hoe was in Chan Master Huangbo's hand. Why was it snatched away by Linji?"

Chan Master Yangshan answered, "Although the one who seized by force was a petty person, his wisdom was superior to that of a gentleman."

Chan Master Guishan again asked Yangshan, saying, "With regard to cultivating and harvesting, why would Linji say this had nothing to do with himself?"

Chan Master Yangshan did not answer, but on the contrary, asked, "Is it not possible to transcend duality?"

Chan Master Guishan, without saying a word, turned around and also went back to the monastery.

The turning around of Chan Master Huangbo, the turning around of Chan Master Guishan, the world of turning around, is the world that affirms everything. People of reason have a lot to say. Those without reason have even more to say. If you are able to turn around in front of truth, is that not another kind of world?

買一片曾田地 又爭叮嚀閱祖翁
綠株度賣未遠 自買多憐松竹引清風

「搶不走」
黄蘖必需清

The Way to Receive Guests

Lord Zhao from the city of Zhaozhou paid a special visit to Chan Master Zhaozhou Congshen. At the time, Chan Master Zhaozhou Congshen was resting on a bed. Lying there, he addressed the visitor and said, "Great Lord! I am already very old. Although you have made a special trip to come see me, I really don't have the strength to get up out of bed to receive you. Please don't be offended."

Not only did Lord Zhao not take offense, on the contrary, he had even more respect for Zhaozhou. The next day, Lord Zhao dispatched a general to present gifts to him. As soon as he heard this, Zhaozhou immediately got out of bed and went outside the door to greet the general.

After this incident, his disciples did not understand, and so asked Chan Master Zhaozhou, "The day before yesterday, when Lord Zhao came, you did not get off the bed. This time, when a subordinate of Lord Zhao came, why did you, on the contrary, get out of bed and go outside the door to receive him?"

Chan Master Zhaozhou explained, saying, "You are unaware of some things. The way I receive guests has three different levels of high, middle, and low. When the first and highest level person comes, I remain on the bed and, using my original face, receive the guest. When the second and middle level person comes, I get off the bed, go to the reception room, and receive him politely. When the third level person comes, I use common social courtesies and go to the front door to welcome him."

Some people take the words "tea," "making tea," "making good tea," or "sit," "please have a seat," "please take the seat of honor" to sneer at the snobbishness of the guest master[45] at temples. In fact, it is not snobbishness. It is just the common etiquette of human relationships. In the ways of the mundane world, of course there are distinctions within the principle of equality. Like Chan Master Zhaozhou's ways of receiving guests, to contemplate and demonstrate different worldly views with the Chan mind is the level of a master. As people conducting our lives in this world, should we follow mundane truth? Supramundane truth? Should we harmonize supramundane and mundane truth? I hope those of you who have the heart will contemplate this!

The Rooster and the Bug

There was a child who was only seven years old. However, he would often seek out Chan Master Wude and talk with him about everything. Nevertheless, Chan Master Wude thought the child's quick wit was extraordinary, for the words that came out of him often had a little bit of Chan flavor. One day, Chan Master Wude said to him, "This old monk is very busy every day. I don't have time to frequently debate and chatter with you. Now, I will debate with you once more. If you lose, you'll have to buy cakes and offer them to me. If I lose, I will buy cakes for you."

After listening to this, the child said, "Then please, Master, take the money out first!"

Chan Master Wude said, "It is most important when one loses a debate; only then do you need the money. If one wins the debate, then it actually isn't an issue. First, let's suppose this old monk is a rooster."

The child said, "I am a little bug."

Chan Master Wude seized the opportunity and said, "Yes, you are a little bug. You should buy a cake for me, this big rooster, to eat!"

The child would not admit defeat and argued, "No way, Master! You should buy the cake for me! You are a big rooster. I am a little bug. When I see you, I can fly away. Because of our master and disciple relationship, we cannot argue! Then, haven't you lost?"

Chan Master Wude grabbed the child's hand and led him to a large crowd of people. Chan Master Wude said, "This issue is similar to war and politics. If a local official cannot make a decision, then we must ask the people to make a ruling. There are three hundred villagers here. Among them, it cannot be said that we do not have any supporters. Everyone! Will you please determine for this old monk and child which one is more reasonable."

The people were unable to decide. Therefore, Chan Master Wude earnestly and solemnly said, "One must be a Chan master with eyes opened to be able to judge this."

Three days passed. Only then did all the people in the monastery notice that Chan Master Wude had secretly bought cakes for the seven-year-old child.

The rooster and the bug–between this pair of old and young Chan practitioners, there must be many more humorous tales.

In Chan, there is no big or small, long or short, right or wrong, good or bad. Of course, in Chan, there is also no losing or winning. From the beginning, Chan Master Wude wanted to triumph over the seven-year-old child. However, the seven-year-old child was willing to be a weak, little bug. When the big rooster stretches out to peck with his beak, the bug is the most appetizing of foods. Yet, the little bug can fly away. This symbolizes that the master and the disciple cannot argue. Chan is a world of no arguing, but Chan is also a world of regularity and order.

Do Not Wipe It Off

There was a young man who was very hot-tempered. Moreover, he liked to fight with others so a lot of people did not like him. One day, he unintentionally wandered into Daitoku Temple.[46] By coincidence, he heard Zen Master Ikkyu giving a Dharma talk. After listening to it, he vowed to repent his past mistakes and said to Zen Master Ikkyu, "Master, I will never again fight or quarrel with other people so as to avoid being disliked by all. Even if someone spits in my face, I will tolerantly wipe it off and silently bear it!"

Zen Master Ikkyu said, "Oh! Why bother? Just let the spit dry by itself. Don't wipe it off!"

"How is that possible? Why do I have to endure it like that?"

"This isn't about being able to or not being able to endure. You just treat it as a mosquito or an insect resting on your face. It's not worth fighting with it or scolding it. Although you are spit upon, that is actually not an insult. Accept it with a smile!" Ikkyu said.

"If the other party doesn't spit, but uses his fists to strike you, then what do you do?"

"The same! Don't take it too much to heart. It's only a punch after all."

Hearing this, the young man thought what Ikkyu had said was totally unreasonable. Finally, unable to control himself, he suddenly raised his fist, struck Zen Master Ikkyu on the head, and asked, "Monk, how about now?"

The Zen Master said in a very concerned manner, "My head is as hard as a rock. I didn't feel much. On the contrary, your hand probably hurts from hitting me!"

The youth was dumbfounded and could not say anything.

In this world—no matter what it is—talking about it is easy; doing it is very difficult. We talk about not getting angry, but when circumstances arise, we cannot control ourselves. A Chan practitioner said, "When talking, it seems like we are enlightened; when facing conditions, delusions arise." This is such a description.

説時似悟　對境生迷
心境自轉　方法正道

不要掃試

一休禾信徒

-71-

The Beggar and Chan

The wandering monk Tosui was a famous Zen master who had lived at quite a few Chan monasteries. It could be said that he was highly cultivated and well learned. He had taught Chan to people at various places.

As a result, the Chan monastery of which he was abbot had attracted too many monastics and students. However, these students often were unable to endure the hardships and the arduous work. Halfway through, they would give up. He had no choice but to declare that he was resigning his position, and he advised them to disperse and go their own way. From then on, no one could discover Zen Master Tosui's whereabouts.

Three years later, one of his disciples found him under a bridge in Kyoto, living with several beggars. This disciple immediately implored Zen Master Tosui to give him instruction.

Zen Master Tosui told him curtly, "You don't have the qualifications to receive my guidance."

The disciple asked, "How can I become qualified then?"

Zen Master Tosui said, "If you are able to live as I do under the bridge for three or five days, I may be able to teach you."

Consequently, this disciple dressed up as a beggar and passed the day with Zen Master Tosui, living as a beggar. The second day, one of the beggars among them died. At midnight, Zen Master Tosui and his student carried the corpse to the mountainside to bury it. After the task was completed, they still returned to their sojourn under the bridge.

Tosui lay down and went to sleep, sleeping straight through till dawn. However, his student could not fall asleep at all. After day had broken, Zen Master Tosui said to his disciple, "Today, we don't need to go out and beg for food. Our dead companion has left some food over there." But the disciple, seeing the filthy bowl, could not even swallow down a mouthful.

Zen Master Tosui said brusquely, "I once said you were incapable of studying with me. This heaven here, you cannot enjoy it. You had better go back to your human world. Please don't tell other people my whereabouts because the inhabitants of the heavens and pure lands don't wish to be disturbed by others."

The disciple cried as he knelt down and said, "Teacher! Please take care of yourself! This disciple really doesn't have the qualifications to study with you because your heaven cannot be understood by him!"

In the eyes of a true Chan practitioner, where are the heavens and pure lands? In menial work, there are heavens and pure lands. In loving people and taking care of things, there are heavens and pure lands. In guiding others and changing conditions, there are heavens and pure lands. So the heavens and pure lands are in the mind of the Chan practitioner, not outside the mind.

Original Face

Chan Master Xiangyan Zhixian was a disciple of Chan Master Baizhang who was well versed in the sutras and commentaries. Later, he studied with his Dharma brother Chan Master Lingyou. One day, Lingyou said to him, "I've heard that you are well-read in a wide range of studies. Now I ask you—'Before my parents gave birth to me, what was my original face?'"

Chan Master Zhixian was stumped for a moment. He returned to his residence, looked through his all books, but still could not find an answer. He again returned to the Chan Master and said, "Venerable, be compassionate. Please instruct me! What is the original face before my parents gave birth to me?"

Chan Master Guishan Lingyou said firmly and clearly, "I can't tell you because if I tell you the answer, it is still mine and has nothing to do with you. If I tell you, you will regret it in the future and might even blame me."

Chan Master Zhixian, seeing that his Dharma brother would not instruct him, sadly burned all of his sutras. From then on, he went to Mt. Ziyai in Nanyang to watch over the tomb of Imperial Master Huizhong. Day and night, he contemplated this question like a mute who had swallowed a ball of fire. One day, while weeding in the fields, his hoe suddenly hit a stone and made a clacking sound. Immediately, his body and mind dropped off[47] and he had a great awakening. Thereupon, he bathed and lit incense. Facing Mt. Gui,[48] he bowed from afar and said, "Venerable, you really are too compassionate. If you had told me in the beginning, I would not have today's joy!"

Chan awakening is not something that is given to us by other people. It requires us to understand with the mind and the spirit.

常勸特似禮西方
何勞特似禮西方
起眉毛頹色稈

令之自己天真佛晝夜六時
《本來面目》
香嚴智
潙山靈祐

The Chan in Tea and Meals

Chan Master Longtan Chongxin of the Tang Dynasty became a monk under Chan Master Tianhuang Daowu. For several years, he chopped firewood and prepared meals, carried water and made soup, but he had never received so much as a word of the essentials of the Dharma from Chan Master Daowu. Therefore, one day, he said to his teacher, "Master, it's been many years since I became a monk under you. Yet, not once have I received instruction from you. Please, Master, be compassionate and teach me the essentials of the Dharma for cultivating the Way."

After hearing this, Chan Master Daowu immediately responded, saying, "What you just said does a very grave injustice to your master! Think about it: ever since you became a monk under me, not a day has passed that I haven't transmitted to you the essential teachings for cultivating the Way."

"Your disciple is stupid and does not know what you've taught and transmitted to him," Chongxin said in astonishment.

"When you bring tea to me, I drink it for your sake. When you bring food to me, I eat it for your sake. When you join palms to show respect to me, I nod my head to you. There hasn't been a day in which I have been remiss. Have I not been instructing you in the essential teachings of the mind all along?"

Upon hearing this, Chan Master Chongxin immediately awakened.

From this exchange between master and disciple, we can understand that Chan is life. In our daily activities—such as hauling firewood, carrying water, drinking tea, or eating food—all are rich in the boundless subtleties of Chan.

Pick Up A Little More

Chan Master Dingzhou and a novice monk were in the courtyard doing walking meditation. Suddenly, a gust of wind blew and many leaves fell down from the trees. The Chan Master then bent over, picked up the leaves one by one, and put them in his pocket. The novice by his side said, "Chan Master, don't pick up anymore. We will sweep early tomorrow morning anyway."

Chan Master Dingzhou took exception to this and said, "You shouldn't talk like that. Do you mean to say that sweeping will make it clean? With each leaf I pick up, it will make the ground a little bit cleaner!"

The novice monk said again, "Chan Master, there are so many fallen leaves. You pick them up now, but more will fall down afterwards. How will you ever finish picking them up?"

As Chan Master Dingzhou was picking them up, he said "The fallen leaves are not only on the ground; the fallen leaves are also on the mind-ground. When I pick up the fallen leaves from the ground of my mind, there will come a time when they are finally all picked up."

After hearing this, the novice monk finally understood what the Chan practitioner's life is about.

During the Buddha's lifetime, he had a disciple named Suddhipamthaka who was very slow-witted. When he was taught a gatha, he could recite the first verse but would forget the next verse, or recite the next verse but forget the verse before. Having no choice, the Buddha asked him what he could do. He said he could sweep the floor. The Buddha then told him to recite the phrase "whisking dust; sweeping dirt" whenever he swept the ground. After reciting this for a long time, he thought: when it is dusty and dirty outside, one must use a broom to sweep it clean; when it is filthy in the mind, how do we sweep it clean?

In this way, Suddhipamthaka gained wisdom.

Chan Master Dingzhou's picking up of the fallen leaves could be better said as picking up the mind's delusions and afflictions. All of the fallen leaves on this great earth—we need not pay attention to them. For each fallen leaf in the mind that we pick up, there is one less. Chan practitioners only need to settle the mind in the moment and then they immediately have everything in this great chiliocosm. Confucians[49] believe in demanding a lot from oneself in everything. Chan practitioners require that when the mind is pure, the land will be pure. Therefore, every person should, at all times and in all places, remove the fallen leaves in their own minds.

鼎州禪師

沙彌

佛國好景絕塵埃 煙霧童童郁又開
若見人來閉你齋 一花一葉一如來

One Sitting, Forty Years

Chan Master Foku Weize was a native of Changan during the Song Dynasty.[50] After he became a monk at a young age, he practiced at Foku hut on Cuiping Rock on Mt. Tiantai in Zhejiang Province.

He used fallen leaves to patch the roof and form a grass hut. He took fresh water to moisten his throat. Each day, only at noon, he picked wild fruit from the mountain to fill his hungry belly.

One day, a woodcutter passed by the hut and saw a practicing old monk. Out of curiosity, he came forward and asked, "How long have you lived here?"

Chan Master Foku replied, "About forty years have already passed."

The woodcutter inquisitively asked again, "Are you the only person practicing here?"

Chan Master Foku nodded, saying, "In dense woods, deep in the mountains, one person here is already considered too many. What need is there for more people?"

The woodcutter then asked, "Don't you have any friends?"

Chan Master Foku clapped his hands making a sound, and many tigers and panthers came out from behind the hut. The woodcutter was completely startled. Chan Master Foku quickly told him not to be afraid. After he signaled to the tigers and panthers and they returned behind the hut, the Chan Master said, "My friends are many. The great earth, mountains, and rivers; the trees, flowers, and grass; the insects, snakes, and wild beasts are all my Dharma companions."

The woodcutter was extremely moved. He willingly took refuge and became a disciple. Foku, giving brief instruction to the woodcutter concerning the essence of the Dharma, said, "Today, you are an ordinary person, but you are not an ordinary person. Although not an ordinary person, you do not disturb worldly law."

With these words, the woodcutter understood. From then on, numerous people admiring the Way came. On Cuiping Rock, where white clouds float in the sky, grass and trees welcome people, tigers come and go, deer pass by, birds fly, and insects chirp, they became the Foku branch of the Chan School.

Using common sense to look at "one sitting, forty years," forty years is a very long time. However, to sages who have awakened to limitless time and entered "eternal life," and to Chan Master Weize who had already melted into and entered the great universe, this is only an instant. In the mind of Chan practitioners, there is actually no difference between an instant and forty years.

In a Chan practitioner's awakening to the Way, what he awakens to is that there is no difference in time and space, no differentiation between other and self, no distinction between movement and stillness, and no concept of sentient beings and Buddhas.

"Although you are an ordinary person, you are not the same as ordinary people." Because everyone has Buddha nature, and in truth there is no provisional naming of sentient beings and Buddhas, how can there be any difference between ordinary people and unordinary people? "Although not an ordinary person, you do not disturb worldly law." As Chan practitioners awaken to the Way, they do not destroy but establish another way, and they do not destroy myriad dharmas but instead have already transcended these dharmas.

汝令善听非但支佛但不坏非法坏法佛益唯佛能知《一性の十重》佛益唯则支

A Poem

Chan Master Shuangxi Buna and Chan Master Qisong were good friends. Moreover, they both had already reached a level where they connected with true mind through Chan. One day, Chan Master Qisong playfully commemorated Chan Master Buna, who was still alive and well, with a poem, saying:

Succession of the patriarch should be in our generation,
The conditions of birth follow a pattern;
All his life, he was always with the Way,
Knew he was ill, unwilling to seek treatment.
To describe ancient forms, hard for the pen to express,
This profound feeling, the world does not know;
The compassionate clouds, where do they go?
The solitary moon by itself is carefree.

After Chan Master Buna finished reading Chan Master Qisong's commemorative poem, he very happily picked up a brush and responded:

All my life, who else is in harmony with me on the Way,
But noble you know my innermost heart best;
At first, I did not yet expect to part,
But I fear hindering my fellow practitioner's poem.

After he finished writing, Chan Master Buna immediately tossed his brush aside, sat down, and died.

Originally, Chan Master Buna had no intention of entering nirvana. However, because he cared for the reputation of his Dharma friend's poetry, he entered nirvana. The friendships of Chan masters, in which they willingly sacrifice their lives for each other, are indeed extremely rare.

Ancient people have died to return favors to their very close friends, but that was all done in order to pay a debt of gratitude or for other reasons. Furthermore, for the sake of his Dharma friend's playful words, Chan Master Buna immediately used death to protect his Dharma friend's view. The meaning in Chan Master Qisong's poem is about succeeding and shouldering the Dharma transmission[51] of Chan Master Buna. We can also say it is just a joke, or say it is a poem, or true insight. Chan Master Buna, in order to give his approval, entered nirvana without the least bit of hesitation. People who do not understand even think that Chan Master Buna was driven to death by Chan Master Qisong. In fact, with regard to life and death, the Chan Master had already broken through. As long as he transmits to the right person, he can just pass away. It can be said, that this is being carefree and at ease. What could be more beautiful than this?

与怀素上人书生莫有论
家相和少和末有如生相别
照溪同是一空诗

樱溪布衲题松要僧

Happiness and Suffering

Chan Master Tanzhao gave instruction to his disciples and devotees every day. He could not leave without saying, "Happy! Happy! Life is full of happiness!"

However, one time he fell ill. During his illness, he was constantly yelling, "Suffering! Suffering! So much suffering!"

The abbot heard this and came to reproach him, "Hey! For a monastic who is ill to always be complaining of 'suffering, suffering' does not look good."

Tanzhao said, "Health is happiness, sickness is suffering. This is natural. Why can't we cry, 'suffering'?"

The abbot said, "Remember the time you fell into the water and nearly drowned. Your face didn't even change color. That kind of fearless manner–regarding death as returning–where is that heroic spirit now? You normally say, 'happiness, happiness.' Why is it when you get sick, you say 'suffering, suffering'?"

Chan Master Tanzhao said to the abbot, "Come, come. Come to the foot of my bed!"

The abbot went to the side of the bed. Chan Master Tanzhao asked him softly, "Abbot, you just said that I used to say 'happiness, happiness!' Now all I say is 'suffering, suffering!' Please tell me, is saying 'happiness 'correct? Or, is saying 'suffering' correct?"

Life has the two faces of suffering and happiness. When there is too much suffering, we should, of course, give rise to an inner happiness. When there is too much happiness, we should also understand the truth of suffering in life. Intense happiness will give rise to sorrow. Deep suffering causes life to lose its flavor. It is best to live a life of the Middle Way, not attached to suffering and not attached to happiness.

苦時提起快樂　樂時明白苦相
人生苦樂相滲應遇中道生活

《快樂（痛苦）》

Self-liberating Person

Chan Master Huangbo had left home as a child to become a monk. One time, when he made a trip to Mt. Tiantai, he ran into a fellow practitioner whose behavior was unusual. The two of them talked and laughed just like old friends. When they reached the edge of a small stream, the water in the stream just so happened to rise sharply. The fellow practitioner called on Huangbo to cross the river together. Huangbo then said, "My dear friend, the water in the stream is so deep. Can it be crossed?"

The fellow practitioner subsequently lifted his pant legs and crossed the river as naturally as if he were walking on level ground. As he walked, he turned his head back and said, "Come! Come!"

Huangbo then shouted, "Hey! You self-liberating fellow! If I had known earlier that you were like this, (had known you were a self-liberating practitioner with supernatural powers), then I would have broken your heels."

The fellow practitioner whom he had scolded was moved and sighed, "You really are a great vessel of the Dharma. In fact, I am not equal to you!"

Speaking, he then vanished.

Buddhism is divided into the Great Vehicle and the Small Vehicle. The Small Vehicle stresses self-liberation. The Great Vehicle emphasizes liberation of others. Sages who only focus on self-liberation, even if they attain the Way, still are not comparable to practitioners who have made the vow to liberate others. With the style of, "Even if pulling out one hair could help the world, I won't do it!" one cannot ever become a Buddha. "You, yourself, are not yet liberated; you first liberate others–this is the bodhisattva vow." Huangbo reprimanded the self-liberating fellow; it's no wonder the sage was moved, and moreover, sang the praises of the great vessel of the Dharma.

自從大士住
須有圓珠
心印有圓珠
七尺身
樹旁場十畝
棲霞嵐和
雲林今日
法淨賓

《自在漢》
黃藥對償

A Place for Living in Seclusion

Chan Master Wude always traveled far and wide to study and learn. One day, he came to the place where Chan Master Foguang lived. Chan Master Foguang said to him, "You are a very famous Chan practitioner. It's too bad! Why not find a place to live in seclusion?"

Chan Master Wude helplessly answered, "Where exactly is my place for living in seclusion?"

Chan Master Foguang said, "Although you are a very good elder Chan master, you don't even know a place of seclusion."

Chan Master Wude said, "I have ridden horses for thirty years. I never thought I would be thrown off by a donkey today."

Chan Master Wude settled down at Chan Master Foguang's place. One day, a student monk asked, "Away from the study of Buddhist doctrine and terminology, please Chan Master, help me decide!"

Chan Master Wude told him, "That kind of person will be fine."

The student monk was just about to bow, when Chan Master Wude said, "Good question! Good question!"

The student monk said, "At first, I wanted to ask the Chan Master, but...."

Chan Master Wude said, "I will not answer today!"

The student monk asked, "When it is so clean it does not even have a speck of dust, then what?"

Chan Master Wude answered, "This place of mine does not keep that kind of guest."

The student monk asked, "What is your style of teaching, Chan Master?"

Chan Master Wude said, "I won't tell you."

Unsatisfied, the student monk demanded, "Why won't you tell me?"

Chan Master Wude also bluntly replied, "This is my style."

The student monk even more earnestly demanded, "Your style doesn't even have one word?"

Chan Master Wude said, "Sit and meditate!"

The student monk retorted, "The beggars on the street, aren't they all sitting?"

Chan Master Wude took out a coin and gave it to the student monk.

The student monk finally awakened.

When Chan Master Wude next saw Chan Master Foguang, he reported, "When traveling and studying, travel and study. When living in seclusion, live in seclusion. Now, I have already found a place for living in seclusion!"

Since ancient times, some Chan monks have traveled like clouds and water. Some have lived in seclusion. Some, wishing to hide from the burden of fame, have entered into the mountains only fearing that they were not in deep enough. Some have received people from the ten directions, waiting for the person destined to receive transmission. In fact, what is the Chan monk's true behavior and conduct? Just as Chan Master Wude said, "When traveling and studying, travel and study. When going into hiding, go into hiding."

Huike's Settled Mind

Chan Master Shenguang Huike, traveling over mountains and valleys, arrived at Mt. Song's Shaolin Temple to pay his respects to Patriarch Bodhidharma. He requested instruction and also asked to be taken in as a disciple. Bodhidharma, facing the wall, sat in silent meditation and ignored him. Shenguang, therefore, stood outside the door waiting as the wind and snow blew everywhere. After a long time, the snow was so deep that it was up to his knees. Seeing that he was truly sincere in seeking the Dharma, Bodhidharma then asked, "You have been standing in the snow for a long time. What is it that you seek?"

Shenguang said, "My only wish, Venerable, is that you open the gate of the sweet dew[52] and universally liberate all beings."

Bodhidharma said, "The supreme and wondrous Way of the Buddhas, despite vast kalpas of dedication and diligence, being able to practice what is difficult to practice, being able to endure what is difficult to endure, still cannot be attained. You, sir, with your frivolous and arrogant heart, longing and hoping for the true vehicle, toil in vain."

Shenguang, hearing this encouraging instruction,[53] immediately cut off his arm with a knife in front of Bodhidharma.

Bodhidharma said, "All Buddhas seeking the Way for the sake of the Dharma, disregard their physical form. Now that you have cut off your arm, what else are you seeking?"

Shenguang answered, "Your disciple's mind is not yet settled. Please, Patriarch, settle the mind for me!"

Bodhidharma shouted, "Bring forth the mind. I will settle it for you!"

Dumbfounded, Shenguang said, "I cannot find the mind!"

Bodhidharma smiled and said, "I have already settled the mind for you."

Shenguang Huike was at the point of not finding; then there was a turning around and entry. Finally, he had a clear and great awakening. Our afflictions are originally empty; unwholesome karma has no intrinsic nature. The place where the mind attains the state of nirvana, where there are no delusions and no arising of thought, is supreme enlightenment. This is the Buddha Way. If you are able to preserve a true mind of equanimity, your Buddha nature will be revealed at that moment.

Treasure the Present

When Master Shinran of Japan was nine years old, he was already determined to become a monk. He requested that Zen Master Jichin tonsure him. Zen Master Jichin then asked him, "You're still so young. Why do you want to renounce home life and become a monk?"

Shinran said, "Although I am just nine years old, my father and mother have already passed away. Because I don't know, why must people die? Why must I be separated from my father and mother? Therefore, in order to investigate this level of truth, I must become a monk."

Zen Master Jichin highly praised his aspirations, saying, "Good! I understand now. I am willing to receive you as my disciple. However, it's already too late today. Wait until tomorrow morning, then I will tonsure you!"

After Shinran heard this, he strongly objected saying, "Master! Although you say you will tonsure me early tomorrow morning, I am, after all, young and ignorant and can't guarantee whether my determination to become a monk will last until tomorrow. Besides, Master, you are so old. You can't guarantee whether you will still be alive tomorrow morning when it is time to get out of bed."

Zen Master Jichin, after hearing these words, clapped his hands in applause. And, with a heart full of joy, said, "Correct! What you say is absolutely correct. Now, I will immediately tonsure you!"

When Venerable Master Xuanzang of the Tang Dynasty became a monk at twelve years old, Tang Dynasty monastics were required to take and pass an exam.[54] At that time, Xuanzang was young and could not yet be accepted. Xuanzang was brokenhearted and wept bitterly. The head examiner Zheng Shanguo asked why he must become a monk. Xuanzang answered with, "Bring glory to the teachings of the Tathagata and propagate the bodhi seeds of the Buddha."[55] Because his aspirations were great, he was given special permission to become a monk. These two sages of China and Japan, reflecting on one another and shining through the ages, have also become inspirational stories of Buddhism today.

佛說三世佛法現在最珍惜
過去不可追未來猶難料

《珍惜現在》
慈鎮敬繪親鸞

Speaking of the Supreme Dharma

Chan Master Foguang brought up a gongan to a student monk, saying:

In ancient times, most people used paper lanterns with candles to light up the road. One day, a blind person paid a visit to one of his friends. When he was taking his leave, because the sky was already dark, his friend gave him a lantern to light his way home.

The blind one politely declined his friend's kindness, saying, "I don't need a lantern. No matter whether it is light or dark, it is all the same to me."

The friend explained, "I know you don't need a lantern to light your way home. But, if you don't carry a lantern, other people might run into you. Therefore, you better still take it."

The words he spoke sounded reasonable, so this blind person took the lantern and went back home. But, he had not gone far when someone ran right into him. The blind one scolded the other person, saying, "Look where you're going! Can't you see the lantern in my hand?"

Besides offering an apology, the wayfarer said, "My dear fellow, your candle is already extinguished."

The blind one said, "It's the light of your mind that has been extinguished. What does that have to do with my candle going out?"

To people who see their nature, bright prajna and dark ignorance are the same. There is no difference. Although dark afflictions cause people to suffer, does not the brightness of the scorching sun also burn people? Even though this is the case, why not employ compassionate means, raising a torch of wisdom to illuminate and reveal the light in the minds of all sentient beings?

Sentient beings, from beginningless time, have had deep and strong attachments to the self. Birth and death, death and birth: the long night is very dark. Although he has two eyes, yet he cannot see the person on the road right before his eyes. When blaming the blind man's lantern for being extinguished, he had his eyes open, but did not use his mind. Only the extinguishing of the light of the mind is more lamentable. For example, everyday people who have not yet understood the great meaning of the Dharma misinterpret the Dharma and slander the Triple Gem everywhere. This is like a seeing person running into a blind man's lantern. How can you still blame the lantern for not being lit?

鹿有巖敞千花糊火乾不眼風蟲
人三門戶眼晄火坤寒眼月蟲

The Most Charming

There was once a female patron of Buddhism whose family was very wealthy. Whether it was her riches, social status, abilities, power, and outward beauty, no one could compare. However, she still felt low-spirited and unhappy. She did not even have anyone to have a heart-to-heart with. Therefore, she went to Chan Master Wude to ask for instruction on how to become charming in order to win the admiration of others.

Chan Master Wude told her, "If you are able to cooperate with all kinds of people at all times and in all places, and also have compassion like that of the Buddhas in your heart, speak some Chan words, hear some Chan sounds, do some Chan deeds, apply the Chan mind, then you can become a charming person."

After the female patron heard this, she asked, "How are Chan words spoken?"

Chan Master Wude said, "Chan words are speaking joyful words, speaking true words, speaking modest words, speaking words that benefit others."

The female patron then asked, "How are Chan sounds heard?"

Chan Master Wude said, "Chan sounds transform all sounds into wondrous sounds, taking scolding sounds and turning them into compassionate sounds, taking slanderous sounds and turning them into helpful sounds. Crying sounds, noisy sounds, crude sounds, ugly sounds–when you can pay no mind to all of these, then that is the sound of Chan."

The female patron then asked, "How are Chan deeds done?"

Chan Master Wude answered, "Chan deeds are acts of charity, acts of benevolence, acts of service, acts that are in accordance with the Dharma."

The female patron took it one step further and asked, "How is the Chan mind applied?"

Chan Master Wude said, "The Chan mind is the mind of you and me as one, the mind where sacred and ordinary are one and the same, the mind that embraces everything, the mind that universally benefits everything."

After the female patron listened to this, she completely changed from her former arrogance. In front of others, she no longer flaunted her wealth and never again presumed upon her own beauty. Towards others, she was always respectful and courteous. Towards her family especially, she showed considerate and sympathetic concern. Before long, she was praised as "the most charming patron."

Chan is not theory. Chan is life. When there is Chan in life, then the power of the Dharma is boundless, you will be respected by everyone, you will be valued everywhere. When there is Chan, everything you do in life will be successful.

恭敬喜禪音柔和悅禪事慈悲善心是名真莊嚴

《最具魅力》
無德對女施主

Like Cow Dung

Su Dongpo of the Song Dynasty went to Jinshan Temple to practice meditation and contemplate Chan with Chan Master Foyin. Su Dongpo felt his body and mind flowing freely, so he asked the Chan Master, "Chan Master! When you look at my manner of sitting, what do you think?"

"Very dignified, like a Buddha!"

Hearing this, Su Dongpo was very pleased. Chan Master Foyin then asked Su Dongpo, "Scholar! When you look at my sitting posture, what do you think?"

Su Dongpo, never passing up an opportunity to mock the Chan Master, immediately replied, "Like a pile of cow dung!"

Hearing this, Chan Master Foyin was also very delighted! When the Chan Master was compared to cow dung and surprisingly could not respond, Su Dongpo thought to himself that he had triumphed over Chan Master Foyin. Therefore, he told whomever he came across, "I won today!"

When the news reached the ears of his little sister, Su Xiaomei, she asked, "Older brother! How, exactly, did you defeat the Chan Master?" Su Dongpo was beside himself with joy. In high spirits, he related the facts one more time. Su Xiaomei's natural gifts surpassed that of others and she was of uncommon brilliance. After listening to Su Dongpo's self-satisfied narration, she sternly said, "Older brother, you lost! The Chan Master's mind is like the Buddha's. Therefore, he saw you as a Buddha. But your mind is like cow dung. Therefore, you saw the Chan Master as cow dung!"

Su Dongpo was dumbstruck. Just then, he realized his own Chan attainment was not as good as that of Chan Master Foyin.

Chan is not knowledge; it is awakening to one's nature. Chan is not clever debate; it is spiritual wisdom. Do not think that the exchanges of Chan masters are always sharp. Sometimes, they are silent and do not speak. They do not communicate through spoken language and written words, yet they have the same earsplitting Dharma sounds.

如禪心佛視人如亦佛視人如人心如亦佛視人

佛印東坡

牛糞象糞

Abnormal

There was a devotee who said to Zen Master Mokusan, "My wife is avaricious and miserly. With regard to good deeds, she won't give up one penny. Can you be so compassionate as to go to my home and instruct my wife on doing some good deeds?"

Mokusan very compassionately consented.

When Mokusan arrived at the devotee's home, the devotee's wife came out to greet him. However, she was reluctant to offer him even one cup of tea. The Zen Master made a fist and said, "Madam, look at my hand. If it were like this every day, what would you think?"

The Madam said, "If the hand were like that every day, it has a problem. An abnormality!"

"This is abnormal!" Then, Zen Master Mokusan stretched open his hand and asked, "Suppose the hand were like this every day then?"

The Madam said, "That is also abnormal!"

Zen Master Mokusan immediately said, "Madam, that is correct! These are all abnormal. Only knowing how to hoard money and not knowing how to give charity is abnormal. Only knowing how to spend money, not knowing how to save, is also abnormal. Money should circulate. It should come in and go out, and expenses should be regulated according to income."

The wife, under the guidance of Zen Master Mokusan's analogy, clearly understood how to conduct herself and manage affairs as well as the concept of finances and the way of using her wealth!

In this world, there are people who are extremely avaricious and people who are overly generous. Both are not in accordance with the meaning of the Middle Way in Buddhism. Greedy people should know that joyful giving and forming a connection with others are causes for making money and things going smoothly. If you do not sow the seeds, how can you reap a harvest? People who give charity should do so under conditions that do not cause themselves trouble or anxiety. Otherwise, it becomes impure charity. Zen Master Mokusan's using his hand as an analogy had profound truth in it.

求名空自惜
名利二字陷人坑
真須避远娘生面
一片灵心是觉皇

-101-

Question and Answer in the Chan School

When Chan Master Dongshan met with Head Monk Chu, the Head Monk said, "Too wonderful! Too wonderful! The world of the Buddha Way is so profound it cannot be known."

Chan Master Dongshan therefore asked, "Regarding whether the world of the Buddha Way can or cannot be fully fathomed, let's not talk about that for the time being. Now, just let me ask you, person who speaks of the world of the Buddha Way, exactly what world is that person from?"

Head Monk Chu was silent and did not answer. Chan Master Dongshan asked more persistently, "Why don't you answer me quickly? Tell me! Which world are you from?"

Head Monk Chu said, "You shouldn't be so rash and impatient!"

Chan Master Dongshan said, "You didn't even answer my main point. How can I not be rash and impatient?"

Head Monk Chu still did not answer. Chan Master Dongshan continued to ask persistently, "Whether it is the 'Buddha' or the 'Way,' it is just a name. Then why don't you speak by quoting the sutras?"

As soon as Head Monk Chu heard this, he enthusiastically asked, "What do the sutras say?"

Chan Master Dongshan replied, "In the sutras, the Four Reliances speak of relying on the meaning, not the words. The meaning is: as long as the significance is firmly grasped, you don't need to differentiate between the words."

Head Monk Chu, taking exception to this, said, "You are still creating a disease in the mind based on the sutras!"

Chan Master Dongshan said, "Your illness of arguing that the world of the Buddha Way cannot be fully fathomed; this sickness of passive ineptitude and an unwillingness to directly take responsibility—what about it?"

Now, Head Monk Chu was once again silent. This was not not answering. This was already not being able to answer. The next day, someone said that Head Monk Chu had suddenly died. Therefore, the Chan practitioners of the day all called Dongshan "the Chan Master Liangjie who questioned Head Monk Chu to death."

It is very hard to determine whether there was any real relationship between the sudden death of Head Monk Chu and the persistent questioning of Chan Master Dongshan Liangjie. However, the question and answer of the Chan School is truly like sparks from flint or flashes of lightning. It is so fast it does not allow you to differentiate: "With just one blink of an eye, the hen becomes a duck." The world of the Buddha Way does not allow discussion of its deepness or shallowness. Therefore, beyond this so-called deep and shallow, within and without, is there still differentiation or not?

禅月容谷
深不可测
快如电光
不佇分别

《禅關問答》
洞山□首座

Niaoke and Bai Juyi

One day, the literary giant Bai Juyi paid a visit to Chan Master Niaoke Daolin. He saw the Chan Master sitting upright[56] by a magpie's nest, so he said, "Chan Master, living in a tree is too dangerous!"

The Chan Master replied, "Magistrate, it is *your* situation that is extremely dangerous!"

Bai Juyi heard this and, taking exception, said, "I am an important official in this imperial court. What danger is there?"

The Chan Master said, "The torch is handed from one to another, people follow their own inclinations without end. How can you say it's not dangerous?" The meaning is to say that in officialdom, there are rises and falls, and people scheming against one another. Danger is right before your eyes. Bai Juyi seemed to come to some sort of understanding. Changing the subject, he then asked, "What is the essential teaching of the Dharma?"

The Chan Master replied, "Commit no evil. Do good deeds!" Hearing this, Bai Juyi thought the Chan Master would instruct him with some profound concept. Yet, they were just ordinary words. Feeling very disappointed, he said, "Even a three-year-old child knows this concept!"

The Chan Master said, "Although a three-year-old child can say it, an eighty-year-old man cannot do it."

Although this "Gatha of the Seven Ancient Buddhas" looks trivial and ordinary, how many people are able to accomplish it? If everyone could refrain from evil, and moreover, actively do good, where would there still be evil in the human realm? How could society not be filled with love and joy? Since Bai Juyi listened to the Chan Master's words, he completely changed his egotistical and arrogant attitude.

The Eight Winds Cannot Move Me

Su Dongpo of the Song Dynasty held a government post in Guazhuo, located in Jiangbei, which was only separated from Jinshan Temple in Jiangnan by the Yangzi River. He and Chan Master Foyin, abbot of Jinshan Temple, often conversed about Chan and debated the Way. One day, Su Dongpo, feeling that his cultivation had attainment, composed a poem and dispatched his young attendant across the river to deliver it to Chan Master Foyin for his approval. The poem said:

> Bowing, Heaven within Heaven,
> A light[57] that illuminates the boundless universe,
> The eight winds[58] cannot move me,
> Sitting mindfully upon the purple golden lotus.

After the Chan Master received it from the hands of the young attendant and read it, he took a brush and wrote a one-word comment. He then summoned the young attendant to take it back. Su Dongpo, thinking that the Chan Master would surely praise the state of his cultivation and Chan practice, hurriedly opened the Chan Master's written comments. As soon as he looked, he only saw the word "fart"[59] written on it. The uncontrollable fire of anger began to rise, so he took a boat across the river in search of the Chan Master to debate with him.

When the boat was nearing Jinshan Temple, Chan Master Foyin was already standing on the shore waiting for Su Dongpo. As soon as Su Dongpo saw the Chan Master, he said, panting with rage, "Chan Master, we are the closest of Dharma friends. My poem, my cultivation–if you don't praise it, that's fine. But how could you insult me?"

The Chan Master, acting as if nothing had happened, said, "How did I insult you?"

Su Dongpo took the one-word comment, "fart," written on the poem and showed it to the Chan Master.

The Chan Master roared with laughter and said, "Oh! Didn't you say 'the eight winds cannot move me?' How come 'a fart has knocked you across the river'?"

Su Dongpo was terribly ashamed.

Cultivation is not something you talk about. Doing it is the real accomplishment.

横看成岭
侧成峰
远近高低
各不同
不识庐山
真面目
只缘身在
此山中

《八风吹不动》
佛印对苏东坡

A Mind without the Way

Bundo was a wandering monk. Because he had long admired Zen Master Fugai Ekun's style of practice, he climbed mountains and waded through waters without regard to the long distance until he arrived in front of the cave where the Zen Master dwelled. He said, "The humble student Bundo, having always admired the Zen Master's noble character, has made a special trip to be close to you and wait upon you. Please Venerable, compassionately instruct me!"

Since the hour was already late, Zen Master Ekun said, "The day is coming to an end. Stay here for the night."

The next day, when Bundo awoke, Zen Master Ekun had already gotten up and cooked rice porridge. As they were about to eat, there was not an extra bowl in the cave for Bundo to use. Zen Master Ekun handily picked up a skull from outside the cave and filled it with porridge for Bundo. When Bundo hesitated, not knowing whether to take it, Zen Master Ekun said, "You have the mind without the Way. You didn't really come for the sake of the Dharma. You use deluded feelings of clean and dirty, hate and love to handle situations and receive things. How can you attain the Way?"

Good and evil, right and wrong, gain and loss, clean and dirty—these are from a world that recognizes the differentiating mind. The true Way does not think of good, does not think of evil, is not in purity, is not in impurity. Bundo's thoughts of hate and love, his way of rejecting and accepting, should, of course, be reprimanded for having the mind without the Way.

Poems and Gathas to Debate the Way

When Su Dongpo was living at Donglin Temple on Mt. Lu, he composed a four-line verse. The poem said:

> The babbling creeks are the broad, long tongue;
>
> The scenic mountains are nothing but the pure body.
>
> Nightfall brings eighty-four thousand gathas,
>
> In days ahead, how to present them to others?

The first two lines of this poem, awe-inspiring and deep, are truly amazing.

One day, Chan Master Zhengwu went to have an audience with Chan Master Jingyuan. The two of them chatted into the night. Zhengwu then brought up Dongpo's "Donglin Gatha" and, praising it, said, "This is also a state that is not easy to reach!"

Jingyuan did not agree and criticized, "This kind of statement still has not seen the path. How can it be said that the destination has been reached?"

Zhengwu said, "'The babbling creeks are the broad, long tongue. The scenic mountains are nothing but the pure body.' If that kind of state has not yet been reached, how can it have this message?"

Jingyuan said, "He's just a man outside the gate."[60]

Zhengwu said, "Venerable, be compassionate! Can you point it out?"

Jingyuan said, "From now on, diligently contemplate and break through. Then you can know where your original destiny falls."

After Zhengwu heard this, he completely drew a blank. In deep contemplation the entire night, he could not fall asleep. Without him being aware of it, day had broken. Suddenly, hearing the sound of the bell, he came to a great awakening. The clouds of doubt having disappeared, he said:

> Scholar Dongpo was too loquacious,
>
> In the barrier of sound and form, wishing to reveal the body.
>
> If the stream is sound, the mountain is form,
>
> No mountains, no water–isn't it very lamentable?

Taking this gatha, he ran to tell Chan Master Jingyuan. Jingyuan said, "I told you, he's a man outside the gate!"

Chan is not something that can be spoken of using language, and it is not something that can be written using words. Furthermore, it is not something that can be contemplated with thoughts. Only through awakening can we experience and realize Chan. During Chan Master Zhengwu's night of deep contemplation, the sound of the bell finally struck open the door of his mind. His state and Dongpo's state, then, are not the same.

東坡居士
太鎔音聲
色聞中欲
遠身後是
参山是真
言山翠
水好禪
人

一詩渴禪道
庵元示證悟

I Want Eyeballs

When Chan Master Yunyan was weaving straw sandals, Chan Master Dongshan passed by and upon seeing him, said, "Teacher, can I ask you for one thing?"

Chan Master Yunyan answered, "Tell me and we shall see."

Dongshan rudely said, "I want your eyeballs!"

Chan Master Yunyan very calmly replied, "Want eyeballs? What about your own eyeballs?"

Dongshan said, "I don't have eyeballs!"

Chan Master Yunyan said with a faint smile, "If you had eyeballs, how would you settle them?"

Dongshan had no words to respond with.

Only at this time did Chan Master Yunyan very sternly say, "I think the eyeballs you want should not be my eyeballs, but your own eyeballs!"

Chan Master Dongshan changed his tone of voice again and said, "Actually, what I want are not eyeballs."

Chan Master Yunyan could no longer stand this contradictory manner of speaking, so he shouted at Chan Master Dongshan, "You! Get out!"

Chan Master Dongshan really was not surprised, yet he still said very sincerely, "I can leave. It's just that I don't have eyeballs and can't clearly see the road ahead of me."

Chan Master Yunyan touched his own heart and said, "Didn't I give this to you long ago? How can you still say you can't see?"

Chan Master Dongshan finally awakened with these words.

Chan Master Dongshan asking for eyeballs from other people is a very strange matter. Even someone as clever and wise as Chan Master Yunyan could only tell him in the beginning that his eyes were growing on his own head; why ask others for them? Eventually realizing that what Dongshan wanted was not the physical eyes, Chan Master Yunyan hinted at the wondrous way of the mind's eye. Only then did Dongshan have an awakening.

Physical eyes are that which look upon the world's myriad phenomena: long, short, square, circle, blue, red, maroon, white. This kind of looking is only superficial and phenomenal, with arising and extinguishing. However, only the mind's eye is able to see and observe the essence of all phenomena in the universe. This kind of observing is universal, and has no differentiation within and without. It is no wonder that, although Dongshan had physical eyes, he still could not clearly see the road ahead of him. This road is your original face. It is the goal of becoming a Buddha and a patriarch. When Yunyan told him about the wondrous function of his mind's eye, Dongshan had an awakening.

心眼妙道觀察有慧遍一如無差別
識知未來真面目從佛作祖不為難

要眼珠、雪巖對湄山

－113－

Flowing Out from the Mind

When Chan Master Xuefeng and Chan Master Yantou were traveling together to Mt. Ao in Hunan Province, they ran into snow and were unable to go forward. All day long, if Yantou was not idling away the time, he was sleeping. Xuefeng was always sitting in meditation. He reproached Yantou for only caring about sleeping. Yantou reproached him for only caring about sitting in meditation every day. Xuefeng pointed to his chest and said, "I'm still not steady enough here. How dare I deceive myself and deceive others?"

Yantou was very surprised, his eyes gazing intently at Xuefeng.

Xuefeng said, "Actually, since I began practicing Chan, I have yet to settle my mind!"

Chan Master Yantou felt the opportunity was ripe, so he compassionately instructed, "If this is really the case, tell me what you have seen one by one. What is correct, I will affirm for you. What is incorrect, I will break for you!"

Xuefeng then recounted the course of his own cultivation one time. After Yantou listened to Xuefeng's account, he shouted, "Haven't you ever heard? 'What enters through the door is not the family treasure.'"[61]

Xuefeng then said, "What should I do from now on?"

Chan Master Yantou lowered his voice again, saying, "If you propagate the great doctrines, all your words and deeds must flow out from your mind, and must be performed with integrity and responsibility."

Xuefeng, hearing these words, immediately had a clear awakening.

All worldly knowledge, even science, is comprehended from external phenomena. However, the Dharma is realized from the inner mind and original essence. Xuefeng did not awaken for a long time because, due to myriad external phenomena in the universe, he still had attachments in the mind and was unable to stop his deluded thoughts. "What enters through the door is not the family treasure," which must be able to "flow out from the mind–only that is original nature." This means that we should not study and delve into it from the ends of the branches. We must establish the roots from the fundamental essence.

Big and Small Have No Duality

During the Tang Dynasty, Jiangzhou's Prefect Li Bo asked Chan Master Zhichang, "As is said in the Buddhist sutras, 'Mt. Sumeru contains mustard seeds; a mustard seed embraces Mt. Sumeru.' This is just too unfathomable. A tiny mustard seed–how could it embrace something as large as Mt. Sumeru? It really goes beyond common sense. It has to be a lie, right?"

Chan Master Zhichang heard these words and laughed. He asked, "People say that you've 'read more than ten thousand scrolls.' Is this true?"

"Of course! Of course! How could I have read only ten thousand scrolls?" Li Bo had an air of self-satisfaction about him.

"Then, where are these ten thousand scrolls you've read now?"

Li Bo raised his hand and pointed to his head, saying, "They're all in here!"

Chan Master Zhichang said, "Strange. When I look at your head, it is only as big as a coconut. How can it possibly store ten thousand volumes of books? Can it be that you are lying too?"

After Li Bo heard this, a deafening sound went off in his mind. At that moment, he suddenly had a great awakening.

All dharmas are sometimes explained from phenomena and sometimes comprehended from principle. We have to understand that in this universe, there is principle in phenomena and there are phenomena in principle.[62] "Mt. Sumeru contains mustard seeds" is phenomena. "A mustard seed embraces Mt. Sumeru" is principle. If we are able to understand that principle and phenomena do not obstruct each other, this is completely harmonizing all dharmas.

頃灕藏芥子芥子納須灕
若理事坐礙即圓融諸法

《大小不二》

智常承孝灕

Revere the Bell as a Buddha

The bell in the Buddhist monastery gives the commands. The sound of the bell in the morning is first fast then slow, warning everyone that the long night has already passed and not to continue to indulge in sleep. However, the sound of the bell in the evening is first slow then fast, reminding everyone to be aware of darkness and to alleviate ignorance! Therefore, in the monastery, a day's work and rest begins with the sound of the bell and ends with the sound of the bell.

One day, just as Zen Master Ekido was coming out of samadhi, the melodious sound of the bell drifted over in waves. The Zen Master attentively listened to it with all his heart. When the sound of the bell stopped, he could not help but summon his attendant, inquiring, "Who is the person that was in charge of sounding the bell this morning?"

The attendant replied, "It is a novice monk who has newly come to study."

Then Zen Master Ekido had his attendant send for this novice monk. He asked, "What was your state of mind when you were sounding the bell this morning?"

The novice monk did not know why the Zen Master would ask him this. He responded, "No particular frame of mind! Just struck the bell for the sake of striking the bell."

Zen Master Ekido said, "Is that so? When you were striking the bell, your mind must have been thinking of something because the sound of the bell I heard today was extremely dignified and clear. Only a sincere person with a true mind can produce that kind of sound."

The novice monk thought about it and then said, "Zen Master! Actually, I didn't intentionally think about anything. It's just that, before I left home to become a monk and study, my master often cautioned me: when striking the bell one should think of the bell as the Buddha. One must be pious, purify oneself, revere the bell as the Buddha, have the Chan mind of samadhi, and use a mind of respect to sound the bell."

Hearing this, Zen Master Ekido was very satisfied. Again and again, he reminded, "From now on, when handling affairs, you must not forget to always keep the Chan mind you had when sounding the bell this morning."

This novice monk, from his childhood, had cultivated a habit of respectfulness. Not only when sounding the bell, but in anything he did, any thought he had, he always remembered the instructions of his tonsuring master and Zen Master Ekido to maintain the Chan mind of sounding the bell. He later came to be known as Zen Master Morita Goyu.

Zen Master Ekido not only understood people, but could also tell a person's character from the sound of the bell. This is because he was a person with the Chan mind. As the sayings go, "Whether one has determination or not, just look at how one builds a fire or sweeps the floor" and "Childhood in a glance, reveals old age in part." Although the novice monk Morita was young, even he knew the Chan mind of revering the bell as a Buddha when sounding the bell. It's no wonder that when he grew up, he became a great Chan master! Clearly, if all things had a bit of the Chan mind, what cannot be accomplished?

一年春尽一年春　野草山花笑復新
天晓不因鐘鼓動　月朗非為夜行人

〈敬佛如鐘〉
栗峯沙門森田悟由

Close the Door Properly

There was a thief who made his way into a monastery at night hoping to steal something. However, after rummaging through chests and cabinets, he could not find anything valuable to steal. Having no choice, he was just about to leave when Chan Master Wuxiang, who had been sleeping on the bed, called out, "Hey, Friend! Since you are leaving, please close the door for me on your way out!"

The thief, who was at first taken aback, then promptly said, "So, this is how lazy you are. Even the door has to be closed by someone else. No wonder there isn't anything of value in your monastery."

Chan Master Wuxiang said, "You, my friend, have gone too far. Do you expect this old man to work hard every day to earn the money to buy things for you to steal?"

The thief felt that, encountering such a monk, there really was not a thing he could do.

It was not that the Chan Master did not have anything. What the Chan Master possessed was an inexhaustible treasure that others could not steal. People in the world only know how to accumulate. People would die for wealth, and their minds are burdened by material things. Once you have money, even thieves will not leave you alone. This is not as good as possessing the boundless treasure of wisdom from your original nature. Who can steal it then?

自家本性生限寶藏
瞭□世閒有限財寶

Let Go! Let Go!

There was once a person who took a trip to attend to some business. He had to climb mountains and ford streams, which was very difficult. One time, he was passing by a steep cliff when in a moment of carelessness he fell into the deep ravine. This person saw his life flash before his eyes. With both arms flailing in the air, he happened to grab hold of an old branch of a withered tree on the wall of the cliff, just barely saving his life. However, he was dangling in midair, unable to go up or down. Caught in this predicament and not knowing what to do, he suddenly saw the compassionate Buddha standing on the precipice looking at him kindly. This person, as though seeing some kind of savior, quickly begged the Buddha, "Buddha! I implore you to be compassionate and save me!"

"I can save you, but you must listen to me. Only then do I have a way to help you up," the Buddha said kindly.

"Buddha! In a situation like this, how could I dare not listen to you? Whatever you say, I'll listen to you!"

"All right, then please let go of the branch you're holding onto!"

Hearing this, the person thought, as soon as he let go he would undoubtedly fall into the deep abyss and break every bone in his body. How could he survive? Therefore, he held onto the branch even more tightly and would not let go. The Buddha, seeing this person stubbornly clinging to his delusions, could only leave.

If we want to clarify our mind and see our nature, then we must follow the instructions of the Buddha and let go. When we are on a precipice, only by letting go can we be saved. Otherwise, if we cling with all our might, how can we be saved from dangerous situations?

No Time to Feel Old

Chan Master Foguang's disciple Dazhi, having returned after twenty years of studying and traveling, was in the Dharma hall recounting to Chan Master Foguang his various experiences studying outside the monastery. Chan Master Foguang listened carefully from beginning to end with a comforting and encouraging smile. At last, Dazhi asked, "Teacher! These past twenty years, how have you been?"

Chan Master Foguang said, "Very well! Very well! Teaching, lecturing, writing, and transcribing sutras–I drift along in the ocean of the Dharma every day. In the world, there is no life more joyful than this. Each day, I enjoy being so busy."

Dazhi said in caring tone, "Teacher, you should spend more time resting!"

Late into the night, Chan Master Foguang said to Dazhi, "Go rest! If you have something to say, we can talk about it later."

Early in the morning, in his sleep, Dazhi vaguely heard the intermittent sound of the wooden fish used in chanting coming from Chan Master Foguang's meditation room. During the day, Chan Master Foguang very patiently gave instruction and spoke the Dharma to the groups of devotees and disciples that came to pay respect to the Buddha. As soon as he returned to the meditation hall, if he was not reading and commenting on the reports of student monks, then he was preparing teaching material for devotees. Each day, there were always things to keep him busy.

Finally, seeing a break in the conversation between Chan Master Foguang and the devotees, Dazhi seized the moment. He quickly asked Chan Master Foguang, "Teacher! In these twenty years we've been apart, your daily life is still so busy. How come you don't seem to be getting older?"

Chan Master Foguang said, "I don't have time to feel old."

Later on, this saying, "No time to feel old," continued to echo in Dazhi's ears.

Of the people in the world, some are still very young, but their mind is in decline so they feel old. Some are already old, but their mind is vigorous so they still feel energetic. In old age, they are more robust.

"No time to feel old" actually means that there is no concept of being old in one's mind. As Confucius said, "He is a person who is so eager that he forgets to eat, so joyous that he forgets his worries, and is unaware of the approaching of old age."[63] The Chan practitioner's view of life is also like this.

Once there was an old man whose hair was turning gray. When someone asked about his age, he replied that he was four years old. Everyone was surprised. He said, "For the past seventy years, I lived for myself! The selfish life had no meaning whatsoever. Only in these last four years did I understand how to serve society and people, which I feel is very meaningful. This is why I say I have lived four years."

Not having time to feel old is very good. Otherwise, being a four-year-old old man is also very meaningful.

其為人也發憤忘食樂以忘憂不知老之將至

「沒時間老」描述示大智

A Monastic Robe

There was a Chan Master Wuguo who lived in seclusion in a deep valley wholeheartedly practicing Chan. For over twenty years, a mother and her daughter had supported him with offerings. Because he was still unable to clarify his mind, he was extremely afraid that his practice would be unworthy of the offerings made by devotees. Therefore, he wanted to leave the mountain to seek a teacher and inquire about the Way in order to completely clarify the great matter of life and death. The devout mother and her daughter requested that the Chan Master stay a few more days so they could make a monastic robe for him.

After mother and daughter returned home, they immediately set to work tailoring and sewing. With each stitch, they chanted Amitabha's name. When they finished, they also wrapped up four silver ingots shaped like horse hooves to give to Chan Master Wuguo for his traveling expenses. The Chan Master accepted the goodwill of mother and daughter and prepared to set out down the mountain the next day. That evening, he was still sitting in meditation and resting. Suddenly at midnight, a child dressed in blue clothing and holding a flag followed by several people playing musical instruments and shouldering a very big lotus flower appeared before the Chan Master. The child said, "Chan Master, please ascend the lotus platform!"

The Chan Master pondered to himself, "I've practiced Chan samadhi, but I haven't practiced the Dharma method of the Pure Land School. Even for a practitioner of the Pure Land Dharma method, this state is also unattainable. I fear this is Mara." So, Chan Master Wuguo ignored him. The child urged him again and again not to miss this opportunity. Chan Master Wuguo then grabbed a signal hand bell and stuck it into the lotus platform. Not long after, the child and all the musicians playing their drums and trumpets departed.

Early next morning, just as the Chan Master was setting out, the mother and daughter came bearing a signal hand bell and asked Chan Master Wuguo, "Is this something the Chan Master lost? Last night, our family mare had a stillbirth. The groom used a knife to cut it open and saw this hand bell. We knew this belonged to the Chan Master, so we made a special trip to return it. We just don't know why it came from the horse's belly."

When Chan Master Wuguo heard this, he was drenched in sweat. Then, he composed a gatha:

> A monastic robe, a piece of hide;
> Four silver ingots, four horse hooves.
> If not for this old monk's deep samadhi,
> Nearly became a young foal in your family.

After saying this, he gave the clothes and the silver ingots back to the mother and daughter, bid them farewell, and left!

Buddhist cause and effect and karmic conditions really are unfathomable truths. Even if you are awakened to the Way, if you do not cultivate and attain it, the cycle of birth and death is still difficult to avoid. Looking at Chan Master Wuguo, how can we not be cautious?

龐蘊
贈納衣一張
生の錠元寶の個歸
若非老僧定力深
汝家作馬兒

「一張納衣
無果○母廿護法

No Room for the Ordinary Mind

There was a student monk who went to the Dharma hall to seek instruction from the Chan Master, saying, "Chan Master! I often sit in meditation, regularly chant the sutras, get up early and retire early, and have no distracting thoughts in my mind. I believe there is no one under you more diligent than I, so why am I still unable to awaken?"

The Chan master took a gourd bottle and a handful of raw salt, and gave them to the student monk, saying, "Go fill the gourd with water, pour the salt into it, make it dissolve immediately, and then you will awaken!"

The student monk followed the instructions exactly. Not long after, he ran back and said, "The opening of the gourd is too small. I put the lump of salt in. It didn't dissolve. I stuck a chopstick in. It wouldn't stir. I still cannot awaken."

The Chan master picked up the gourd, poured out some of the water, shook it several times, and the chunk of salt dissolved. The Chan master said kindly, "Being diligent all day long, but not leaving some room for the ordinary mind is like the gourd that is filled with water. It cannot be shaken; it cannot be stirred. How can it dissolve the salt? And how can you awaken?

The student monk said, "Do you mean to say that by not being diligent, you can awaken?"

The Chan master said, "Practice is like playing a zither. Strings that are too tight will break. Strings that are too loose cannot make any sound. The ordinary mind of the Middle Way is the root of awakening."

The student monk finally understood.

Worldly affairs are not advanced through rigid stubbornness. Studying but not applying it can be of no benefit. Leave yourself a little space to turn around. Leave yourself a little time to contemplate. Not hurried, not slow, not tight, not loose—that is the door into the Way.

饥来吃饭倦来眠，热即取凉寒向火，
心心心心道，一世逍遥世是非。
只遮平常心

《死留平常心》
禅师画僧

The Universe as My Bed

One time, Su Dongpo wanted to call on Chan Master Foyin, so he wrote a letter to the Chan Master in advance, telling the Chan Master that, in the same manner Chan Master Zhaozhou had received Lord Zhao, it was not necessary to come out and greet him.

Su Dongpo was confident that he understood the subtleties of Chan, and Chan Master Foyin should receive him with the highest courtesy–receiving by not receiving. However, he still saw Chan Master Foyin run out of the monastery gate to receive him. Finally, seizing the opportunity to make fun of the Chan Master, he said, "Your cultivation is not as carefree as Chan Master Zhaozhou's. I told you not to come and receive me, but you just couldn't ignore social convention, coming all this way to receive me."

Su Dongpo thought that the Chan Master was undoubtedly at a disadvantage this time, but the Chan Master still responded with a gatha, saying:

> Zhaozhou, on that day, was less than modest,
> Not coming out of the monastery gate to receive Lord Zhao.
> How can it be like the boundless form of Mt. Jin,
> The great universe, a Chan bed!

The meaning is: Zhaozhou did not rise from his bed to receive Lord Zhao because Zhaozhou was not modest, not because his state was superior. However, I, Foyin, came out to receive you, but do you think that I have really gotten out of bed? The great universe is my Chan bed. Although you saw me get out of bed to receive you, I am, in fact, still lying on the great universal Chan bed sleeping. You, Su Dongpo, only know about the bed with form that can be seen with the physical eye. Yet, my bed is the vast bed that extends across all space and pervades the dharma realms."

Tone of Voice

There was a student monk who asked Zen Master Bankei for instruction, saying, "I have an innate shortcoming: impatience and shortness of breath. I have been reproached by my master. I also know it is wrong and I need to change it. But, because my impatience has already become a habit, I've never had a way to correct it. Please tell me, Zen Master, do you have any way to help me correct this habit?"

Zen Master Bankei very earnestly replied, "If you can bring out your habit of impatience, I'll help you correct it."

The student monk said, "I'm not impatient right now, but sometimes, it suddenly comes out."

Bankei smiled faintly, saying, "So, if your impatience comes and goes, it's not a habit. Moreover, it's not an innate trait. It arises when you encounter certain situations and does not originally exist. Because of conditions, it arises. If you say your parents gave it to you when you were born, then you are too unfilial. What your parents gave you at birth was only the Buddha mind. Nothing else."

Throughout his life when Zen Master Bankei received students, he did not speak of the Dharma, nor did he speak of Chan. He only asked that each person possess the Buddha mind and a noble character.

Later, after Zen Master Bankei had passed away, a blind person who lived by the monastery said to a student monk who was practicing Chan, "Although I am blind and cannot see the faces of others, I can still determine from someone's tone of voice his personality. Usually, not only can I hear tones of jealousy in a person's words of blessing to those who are happy and successful, but I also can hear tones of self-satisfaction in words of comfort to those who are unfortunate or defeated as if he could gain much benefit from these comforting words. However, in all my experience, Zen Master Bankei's tone of voice when speaking to others was always sincere and unaffected. Whenever he expressed happiness towards people, I only heard the tone of happiness. And, whenever he expressed sorrow, I only heard the tone of sorrow. That kind of tone completely flowed out from his Buddha mind. That Buddha mind was the one given by his parents."

After the student monk heard this, he rejected the blind person's words on the one hand, and praised Zen Master Bankei on the other hand, saying, "Our teacher's Buddha mind was not born from his parents. He had it originally."

By attributing everything good as being born from our parents, we will lose our original nature. By attributing everything bad as being born from our parents, we will also be criticized for being unfilial. Good and bad are habitual tendencies, not original nature. They are neither inherent nor born from our parents. Suppose someone asked, "Who gave birth to the Buddha?" To answer with "The Buddha was born from Queen Maya" is incorrect. Prince Siddhartha was born from Queen Maya, but the Buddha was born from prajna-wisdom. This is what is meant by "Prajna is the mother of all the Buddhas from the three time periods."

盤珪禪師

盤珪佛心不自俱足待人誠氣真誠坐何優

《人的誠氣》
盤珪示學僧

Better Silent than Noisy

One year, during the summer retreat[64] at Lingshu Monastery, King Liu of the Later Han of the Five Dynasties Period[65] insisted on inviting Chan Master Yunmen and the entire community of the monastery to pass the summer in his palace. At the palace, several monks received the court ladies paying their respects and inquiring about the Dharma. The women gathered together chattering pleasantly, so it was very noisy. Especially since King Liu was devout and valued the Dharma, not a day passed without the practice of Chan meditation and lectures. The elders of the monastery were also happy to give Dharma talks to the court ladies and eunuchs. However, only Chan Master Yunmen sat alone meditating silently to the side. As a result, the court ladies did not dare to get close and ask for instruction.

There was an official on duty at the palace who often saw this kind of situation, so he asked Chan Master Yunmen for instruction on the essentials of the Dharma. Chan Master Yunmen always remained silent. Not only was the palace official not offended, he was even more respectful. On the front of Biyu Hall, he posted a poem that said:

> The cultivation of great wisdom begins with Chan,
> In the Chan gate, it is better to be silent, not noisy.
> All the clever ways of speaking, competing for the Truth,[66]
> Still defeated by the "non-speaking" of the Chan gate.

The great masters of the Chan School have always been like leisurely clouds and wild cranes, sometimes dwelling in the mountain forests, sometimes living by the water. With three robes and one mat, they follow their conditions and let things follow their own course. Even when their Dharma conditions are remarkable or they are among royalty, they are not tempted by material gain or moved by power. Just as in Chan Master Yunmen's "a moment of silence, a clap of thunder," even though no words are spoken, his instructions are like thunder rumbling over our heads. If we understand the countless insights in our hearts when we are in silence, then it can be said that we have penetrated a little bit of Chan.

大智修行始是禪
禪門宜默不宜喧

世眼玻璃說事如寒
蠨蜅鄰禪門總不言

《宜默不宜喧》
宜更參禪門

-135-

Grass and Trees Become Buddhas

Zen Master Shinkan of Japan first studied the Tiantai doctrine for six years. Afterwards, he switched to practice Chan for seven years. In order to seek out teachers and inquire about the Way, hoping to clarify the mind and see his nature, and to find his original face, he left home for China's famous mountain monasteries where he contemplated huatou and practiced samadhi for another twelve years.

After more than twenty years, he finally gained insight into his true self through Chan. Therefore, he packed up and returned to his country. In Tokyo, Nara, and other places, he propagated Chan teachings. Scholars and students from everywhere arrived in swarms to practice Chan and seek the Way. They vied with one another, wanting him to answer some difficult questions. Those questions included:

(1) What is our own original face?
(2) What is the true meaning of Patriarch Bodhidharma coming from the West?
(3) When people asked Zhaozhou whether or not dogs have Buddha nature, Zhaozhou sometimes answered, "They do" and sometimes said, "They don't." In fact, do they or don't they?

Although there were many questions, Zen Master Shinkan always kept his eyes closed, not giving an answer. Some people also knew that Zen Master Shinkan was unwilling to discuss Chan gongans with others because no one would gain any real benefit by talking back and forth about gongans.

One day, a Tiantai scholar monk over fifty years of age named Dobun, who had studied the Tiantai doctrine for more than thirty years, came because he admired the Zen Master's reputation. He very sincerely asked, "From my youth, I have studied the Tiantai School's teachings of the *Lotus Sutra*. There is a question I have never been able to understand."

Zen Master Shinkan very straightforwardly answered, "The Tiantai School's teachings of the *Lotus Sutra* are broad and profound, completely harmonious and without obstruction. There should be many questions, and yet, you only have one question you don't understand. What is the question?"

Venerable Dobun asked, "The *Lotus Sutra* says, 'Sentient and non-sentient have the same perfect wisdom.' This meaning suggests that trees, flowers, and grass are all able to become Buddhas. May I inquire, is it really possible for flowers and grass to become Buddhas?"

Zen Master Shinkan did not answer, but asked instead, "For thirty years, you've been thinking about whether or not flowers, grass, and trees can become Buddhas. Of what benefit is this to you? What you should be concerned about is how you, yourself, can become a Buddha. You should think about it like this!"

Venerable Dobun was surprised at first. Then he said, "I've never thought about it in this way before. May I ask then, how do I become a Buddha myself?"

Zen Master Shinkan said, "You said you only had one question to ask me. Regarding the second question, you'll have to solve it yourself."

Can flowers, grasses, and trees become Buddhas? This is not an important question because the great earth, mountains, rivers, flowers, grasses, trees—everything in the universe—all flow out from our intrinsic nature. So long as we become Buddhas, then of course, all grasses and trees will follow to become Buddhas. If we do not investigate the root, but just search the branches, how can we enter the Chan Way?

Chan requires us to immediately recognize our "self" and not to cling to anything else.

-137-

Where Are You From?

When Huineng first met the Fifth Patriarch, the first thing Fifth Patriarch Hongren asked him was, "Where are you from?"

"I come from Lingnan," Huineng replied.

"Lingnan is a place of barbarians. Barbarians don't have Buddha nature!" Hongren said.

Huineng then replied, saying, "People come from the North and the South. Does Buddha nature also have a north and south?"

Because of this important conversation, Fifth Patriarch Hongren held Huineng in especially high regard and, moreover, transmitted his robe and bowl[67] to him.

Later, Sixth Patriarch Huineng also often used the same question to take in and benefit many disciples. Cited below are four instances that illustrate this point:

(1) When Master Shenhui came to study with the Sixth Patriarch, the Sixth Patriarch asked him, "Where are you from?"

Shenhui replied, "I don't come from anywhere."

This answer received the Sixth Patriarch's admiration.

(2) When Chan Master Nanyue Huairang was twenty-three years of age, he paid a visit to the Sixth Patriarch. The Sixth Patriarch also asked him, "Where are you from?"

"I come from Venerable An."

The Sixth Patriarch then asked, "What brings you here?"

Chan Master Huairang was not able to answer this question. Therefore, he lived at Caoxi for more than ten years. He did not awaken until he was over thirty years old.

(3) When Chan Master Qingyuan Xingsi first arrived at Caoxi, the Sixth Patriarch also asked him in this way, "What did you do before you came here?"

Chan Master Xingsi answered him, saying, "I don't even practice the Noble Truths." The meaning is: "I don't even want to become a Buddha or a patriarch. What else do I need do?" These words were also affirmed and highly regarded by the Sixth Patriarch.

(4) Chan Master Nanyang Huizhong was once the Imperial Master of the Tang Dynasty. When he first came to study, the Sixth Patriarch asked him, "Where are you from?"

Huizhong replied, "I come from nearby."

Since the Fifth Patriarch had asked him in the past, "Where are you from?" this consequently opened up the conditions for the Sixth Patriarch to enter the Way. Therefore, when the Sixth Patriarch later received and guided practitioners of Chan, he also used, "Where are you from?" to inspire them, to test them. He wanted them to question the fundamental origin of their own life, to deeply investigate the truth. Raising questions is an important method that the Chan School often uses to connect with one's potential. In these questions and answers, from one to the next, the Chan practitioner finally reflects his own intrinsic nature, recognizing his own original face.

抛却身心現清王 若程不少問行藏
若能識心娘 生而草木叢林尽敢心

The Buddhas Do Not Lie

After Chan Master Huangbo became a monk, he thought, "One must let go of devotion to one's parents. When one attains the unconditioned state, only then can one truly repay debts of gratitude." As a result, he passed the life of a Chan practitioner for thirty years without ever returning home to visit his relatives. However, in his innermost heart, he was very concerned about his aged mother. When he was fifty years old, during one of his travels, he unwittingly walked in the direction of his hometown.

His mother also missed this son who had become a monk, but she had not the slightest bit of news from him. Every day from morning till night, she wept with such sorrow that she lost her eyesight. Because she missed her son, the mother set up a tea stand by the side of the road. Not only did she personally serve the wandering monks who were coming and going, but she also invited them into her home and washed their feet for them to show her respect. Aside from this, there was still another reason: it was because Chan Master Huangbo had a big mole on his left foot. Although she was blind, she hoped that in a one-in-a-thousand chance to wash his feet, she might be able to recognize her beloved son.

On this day, Chan Master Huangbo also accepted his mother's offering. While he was letting his mother wash his feet, he told his mother the story of the Buddha's renunciation. He hoped his mother could gain faith and settle her mind because of it. Chan Master Huangbo would only give his mother his right foot to wash, but he would not let her wash his left foot.

Chan Master Huangbo then returned home a second time. Although he felt it was difficult to leave, he still endured the pain and started on his journey to continue traveling and visiting. The neighbors could not bear the truth and told his mother, "That person who told you the story of Sakyamuni Buddha's renunciation is, in fact, the son you have constantly longed for."

His mother nearly went mad upon hearing this and said, "No wonder that voice was like my son's." Having said this, she then chased after him all the way to the riverbank. As luck would have it, Chan Master Huangbo had already boarded the boat by this time. Moreover, the boat had also set off. The mother desperately jumped into the river and unfortunately drowned.

Standing on the opposite shore, Chan Master Huangbo saw his mother lose her footing, fall into the water, and drown. He could not help the sadness from welling up inside and wept bitterly, saying:

> One son renounces,
> Nine clans of kinsmen ascend to heaven.
> If they do not ascend to heaven,
> The Buddhas tell lies.

After Chan Master Huangbo spoke, he immediately took a boat and returned to cremate his mother. He recited a gatha, saying:

> For many years, my mother's mind was deluded,
> Now a flower blooms in the bodhi forest,
> If we can meet each other again in the future,[68]
> Take refuge in the great compassionate Avalokitesvara.

While Chan Master Huangbo was reciting the gatha, the villagers all saw his mother rise from the flames into the sky and depart.

Chan Master Huangbo Xiyun was a native of Fujian. He became a monk in Jiangxi and received the Dharma from Chan Master Baizhang Huaihai, but he also received the seal of approval from Chan Master Nanquan in Anhui.

Chan Master Huangbo was not an unfilial person. What we call filial piety has three levels: (1) Basic filial piety is to willingly support your parents; (2) Intermediate filial piety is to bring honor to your ancestors; (3) Great filial piety is to liberate the deceased from the cycle of birth and death. The Chan Master's liberating his mother is the greatest demonstration of great filial piety.

一千出泰九族升天若不升天诸佛妄言

《诸佛不欺》
黄檗禅师

A Stick of Incense Increases Merits

Prime Minister Pei Xiu of the Tang Dynasty was a very devout Buddhist. His son, Pei Wende, at a very young age, achieved the highest score in the imperial examination and was appointed as a Hanlin Academy Scholar by the emperor. However, Pei Xiu did not wish for his son to rise to such success so early in life, and to advance as an official at a young age. Therefore, he sent his son to a monastery to cultivate and practice. Furthermore, he wanted him to first do manual labor as a water hauler and fire tender.

This young and successful Hanlin Academy Scholar carried water and chopped firewood at the monastery every day. It made him physically and mentally exhausted, and also extremely vexed. Muttering without end in his heart, he constantly resented his father for sending him to such an old monastery deep in the mountains to be a beast of burden. But because he could not disobey his father's orders, he forced himself to tolerate it. After unwillingly doing this for a period of time, he finally could not stand it, so he complained resentfully:

> Hanlin Academy Scholar, carrying water, sweat dripping to the waist,
> Monk, upon drinking it, how can he take[69] it?

The abbot of the monastery, Chan Master Wude, happened to hear this. With a faint smile, he also recited two verses in response:

> This old monk's one stick of incense,
> Can take on[70] ten thousand kalpas of food.

Pei Wende was shocked. From then on, he disciplined his body and mind, and did the hard labor.

Great people do not sit up on a seat high for others to idolize. Chan practitioners practice what they advocate from doing humble work and performing hard labor to train their willpower. As Mencius said, "Thus, when Heaven is about to confer a great office on a man, it must first strengthen his mind and will, toil his sinews and bones, starve his body, and impoverish the self."[71] Buddhism further emphasizes discipline and laborious training. However, this only enriches the conditions of merit and virtue, which belong to worldly conditioned dharma. Like the Chan Master's stick of incense, the mind can horizontally permeate the ten directions and the nature can vertically penetrate the three time periods. When the mind and nature can correspond with unconditioned dharma, then of course, "This old monk's one stick of incense can take on ten thousand kalpas of food."

翰林挑水
汗淋腰
和尚吃了
焦能消
老僧禪坐一炷
香能消施主
家劫糧

《姓香增福》
散主佳
翰林挑水
🔲🔲

-143-

Where Is There No Buddha?

Once, a Chan master who was in the Buddha Hall chanting with the others suddenly coughed and spat a mouthful of phlegm onto the statue of the Buddha. After the disciplinary monk saw this, he scolded him, saying, "Outrageous! How could you spit phlegm on the Buddha?"

The spitting Chan master coughed again and said to the disciplinary monk, "Please tell me, where in the universe is there no Buddha? Now I am going to spit again. So, may I ask, where is there no Buddha?"

The one who spit had already awakened to the truth, "Buddha nature spreads throughout all space, Dharmakaya fills the universe." You blame me for spitting phlegm on the Buddha, thinking that you are showing respect to the Buddha, but actually, this only shows that you still do not understand what the Buddha is. The Buddha's Dharmakaya spreads throughout all space and fills the dharma realms. Therefore, the Chan master said, "Please tell me, where is there no Buddha?"

When asked this, would you be able to answer? If you cannot answer, then you have not yet awakened to the Way. Even if you are awakened to the Way, when you are asked this in return, your spiritual wisdom and Chan potential will blossom even more from it.

Never Paint Again

Zen Master Gessen was a skilled painting master. However, every time before he did a painting, he would insist that the buyer pay in advance. Otherwise, he absolutely would not lift his brush. This way of doing things was often criticized by the people of society.

One day, a lady requested that Zen Master Gessen do a painting for her. Zen Master Gessen inquired, "How much can you pay?"

"I'll pay however much you want!" the woman answered, "but I want you to come to my house and wield your brush in the presence of my guests."

Zen Master Gessen consented and followed her. As it turned out, the woman was hosting a banquet. Zen Master Gessen used his best brush and did a painting for her. After he finished painting, he took his payment and was about to leave. The lady then said to her guests, "This painter only wants money. Although his painting is very good, his heart is dirty. Money has polluted its beauty. Works from such a filthy spirit are unsuitable to hang in the guest hall. They can only adorn my skirt." As she said this, she took off one of her skirts and wanted Zen Master Gessen to paint on it. Zen Master Gessen asked, "How much will you pay me?"

The lady replied, "Oh, whatever you want." Gessen named an especially high price. Then, according to the woman's demands, he painted a picture. When he finished painting, he immediately left.

Many people questioned why it was all about the money. What was Zen Master Gessen, who did not mind being subjected to any insult, thinking?

The truth was the place where Zen Master Gessen lived often suffered from famine. The rich were unwilling to give money to save the poor. Therefore, he built a granary to store grain for helping the needy. Furthermore, his master had made a vow to build a temple but, unfortunately, died before it was accomplished. Zen Master Gessen wanted to fulfill his master's vow.

After Zen Master Gessen completed these vows, he immediately gave up his brushes and retreated into the seclusion of the mountain forest. From then on, he never painted again. He only had this to say, "When you paint a tiger, you can paint the skin, but it is hard to paint the bones. When you paint a person, you can paint the face, but it is hard to paint the heart." Money is ugly, but the heart is pure.

People with a Chan mind do not haggle over praise or condemnation in this world, like Zen Master Gessen used his artistic talent to save others. His paintings cannot be considered ordinary works of art; they should be considered Chan art. Because he wasn't greedy for money, he was generous with it. But, in the world, how many people are capable of understanding this kind of Chan mind?

The Wondrous Application of Chan

Zen Master Sengai was out spreading the Dharma. On the way, he came across a husband and wife who were arguing.

The wife yelled, "What kind of husband are you? You're not like a man at all!"

The husband retorted, "You curse! If you curse at me one more time, I'll beat you!"

The wife challenged, "I will curse at you. You're not like a man!"

At this time, after Zen Master Sengai had listened to them, he loudly called out to the people passing by, "Come over and see this! To see a bullfight, you have to buy a ticket. To see a cricket fight and a cockfight, you also have to buy tickets. Now there are people fighting, but you don't need to buy a ticket. Come and see!"

The husband and wife still continued arguing. Then the husband said, "If you say *one more time* that I'm not like a man, I'll kill you!"

The wife dared, "Kill me! Kill me! I still say you're not like a man!"

Sengai exclaimed, "How wonderful! Now, for the killing! Come quick and see!"

A passerby shouted, "Venerable! What are you yelling about? A husband and wife are quarreling– what business is it of yours?"

Sengai answered, "How is it none of my business? Didn't you hear that he is going to kill her? If someone is killed, they have to ask a monk to chant sutras. When sutras are chanted, won't I get a red envelope of money?"

The passerby said, "What nonsense! For a red envelope, you would wish for someone to be killed!"

Sengai replied, "Wishing that no one dies is fine too! Then I'll just expound the Dharma."

At this time, even the bickering couple stopped fighting. At the same time, they both gathered around to listen to what Zen Master Sengai and the passerby were quarreling about.

Zen Master Sengai instructed the bickering couple, "No matter how thick the ice is, when the sun comes out, it will melt. No matter how cold the food is, when the firewood is lit, it will be cooked thoroughly. Since conditions bring you together as husband and wife, you need to be the sun that warms the other person, be the firewood that melts the other person. I hope you, husband and wife, will respect and love one another.

This is the way Zen Master Sengai ingeniously applied Chan.

《禅的妙用》
钏尘雀钉妻

互相成熟
彼此温暖
如日如薪
夫妇之道
薪火熟煨
冷硬菜馐
日出都融
壁厚严寒

Doing Evil and Cultivating Goodness

A student monk asked Chan Master Junji for instruction, saying, "What is a person who practices and performs good deeds?"

Chan Master Junji replied, "Those who shoulder pillories and wear chains."

The student monk then asked, "What is a person who does evil?"

Chan Master Junji answered, "Those who practice Chan and enter samadhi."

The student monk said, "Your disciple is ignorant. The Master's instruction is very confusing and difficult to understand. I beseech the Master to use clear and simple words to instruct me!"

Chan Master Junji explained, "So-called evil-doers–the evil do not follow good. Do-gooders–the good do not follow evil."

As if lost in a dense fog, the student monk was still confused. After quite some time, Chan Master Junji asked the student monk, "Understand?"

The student monk replied, "Don't understand."

Chan Master Junji said, "Those who do evil have no good thoughts. Those who do good have no evil mind. Therefore, we say good and evil are like drifting clouds, with nothing born and nothing extinguished."

With these words, the student monk had an awakening.

Speaking of good and evil in the mundane world, we call doing good deeds "goodness," we call doing bad deeds "evil"; goodness has its reward, evil has its retribution. In terms of phenomena, the cause and effect of the three time periods is completely real. However, in terms of original nature, what we call good and evil do not exist. If we are able to not differentiate between good and evil, this we call "seeing the nature," (seeing the original face). This is what is meant by, "Evil, originally empty, is created from the mind. If the mind is extinguished, evil is empty."

Doing good is having shackles and doing evil is called samadhi–we cannot blame the Chan Master for turning it upside down. In terms of the Truth, if we do good deeds but are doggedly attached to worldly and heavenly rewards, is this not being imprisoned by shackles? If we do evil things, although we will transmigrate to the lower realms,[72] our original nature is still the same. Therefore, Chan Master Junji, giving rise to great compassion, presented this profound teaching because he wanted us not to be deluded by good and evil. We should know that when we do good deeds and are reborn into a higher realm,[73] then we attach ourselves to conditioned dharma and take it as the ultimate liberation, this is wrong. When we do evil and fall into the lower realms, then feel discouraged thinking that life is without hope, this is also wrong. The truth is, "good and evil are dharmas, but the Dharma is not good nor evil."

諸惡莫作眾善奉行自淨其意是諸佛教

諸惡莫作眾善奉行自淨其意是諸佛教

-151-

Short-tempered by Nature

When Zen Master Bankei spoke on the Dharma, not only was he very easy to understand but he often allowed devotees to ask questions before the end. Moreover, he would explain them on the spot. As a result, many devotees yearning for the Way came from miles around.

One day, a devotee asked Zen Master Bankei for instruction, saying, "I am short-tempered by nature. I don't know how to correct it."

Bankei asked, "How is this condition 'inborn'? Bring it out and show me. I'll help you get rid of it."

The devotee answered, "No, I don't have it now. As soon as I encounter situations, that inborn impulsive short temper will then rush out!"

Bankei said, "If you don't have it now and it will only appear occasionally in certain situations, that is, when you and other people argue, you create it yourself. Yet now, you say it is inborn, shifting the blame to your parents. Really, this is too unfair."

After this instruction, the devotee understood and never again so easily lost his temper.

Inborn—in the world, there is nothing that is inborn. In nature, causes and conditions coming together will give rise to the myriad phenomena. Our original nature is composed of all good and bad dharmas. This is what is meant by "As mind arises, all dharmas arise; as mind extinguishes, all dharmas extinguish." As long as a person has heart, there is no bad habit that cannot be changed.

罪業本空由心造
心若滅時罪亦亡
心亡罪滅兩俱空
是則名為真懺悔

《永嘉集》
盤珪禪師徒

Where Can We Abide in Peace?

One time, Chan Master Danxia of the Tang Dynasty wanted to call on Chan Master Mazu. On the way, he met an old man with a white beard and a boy with a topknot. Chan Master Danxia saw that the man had an uncommon aura about him, so he stepped forward and respectfully asked, "Sir, where do you live?"

The old man pointed up and down and answered, "Above is heaven; below is earth." His meaning was that, in the universe, everywhere can be home.

As if seizing on a flaw in the old man's statement, Danxia pursued the matter, "What would you do if you were to encounter heaven collapsing and earth sinking?" The meaning is: what would you do if the universe were destroyed?

The old man loudly cried out, "Heaven! Heaven!" meaning that the universe, that heaven and earth, have formation, abiding, decaying, and emptiness.

The boy standing at his side said, "Shhh!" The meaning of this shushing sound was to reveal that the abode of one's original nature is not arising nor extinguished.

Danxia greatly praised them, saying, "Without this father, there wouldn't be this son."

The old man and the boy immediately entered the mountain and were gone.

Abide! Where should we abide? Venerable Cihang said, "As long as we have peace in the mind—north, south, east, or west are all fine." Therefore, above is heaven and below is earth; everywhere is not home, everywhere is home.

However, people of the mundane world dwell in sound, form, material things, and profit; they dwell in fame and power. Since sound, form, material things, profit, fame, and power are all constantly changing, where are we able to safely and peacefully abide?

If we can be sure of ourselves, if we do not allow the five desires and the six dusts to lead us by the nose, and if our minds can be settled, then when heaven collapses and earth cracks, what do we have to fear?

Bodhisattvas, like the pure and clear moon, roam continuously through the ultimate emptiness. When we see the moon in the sky with nothing to support it, it seems really dangerous but is actually very safe. It is because bodhisattvas abide in prajna-wisdom and the nature of emptiness completely without attachments, that they can live at ease.

（理畫圓融派自他

白雲起處毫無痕

海納百川流不斷

空谷萬象任美功題）

The Heart of Chan

The great poet Bai Juyi once asked Chan Master Weikuan, "How can we cultivate body, speech, and mind individually?"

Weikuan answered, "The one with supreme bodhi wears on the body the precepts, speaks from the mouth the Dharma, and practices in the mind Chan. The ways of application are three, but they are one. For example, the rivers Huai and Han have names based on their location. Although the names differ, the nature of the water is not different. The precepts are the Dharma, and the Dharma is not away from Chan. Unite body, speech, and mind to cultivate. Body, speech, and mind are all called the mind. Then why, among them, do we deludedly give rise to differentiation?"

Bai Juyi asked, "Since there is no differentiation, why do we cultivate the mind?"

Weikuan replied, "The mind originally has no flaws, so why do we need to cultivate? You should know, whether it is dirty or pure, all you need is to not give rise to thoughts."

Bai Juyi responded, "Filth—we can wipe away, not giving rise to thoughts of it. Purity—can we not have thoughts about it?"

Weikuan said, "As in our eyes, things cannot remain; specks of gold, though precious, are still harmful in the eye. Black clouds cover the sky; white clouds, likewise, cover the sky."

Bai Juyi continued, "Without cultivation and without thoughts, how are we different from the ordinary person?"

Weikuan answered, "The ordinary people grow in ignorance; the sravaka and pratyeka-buddhas still have attachments.[74] Staying away from these two diseases of ignorance and attachment is called true cultivation. The true practitioner must not be diligent and must not be neglectful. Those who are diligent are close to attachment; those who are neglectful fall into ignorance. This is the heart of Chan."

Bai Juyi had an awakening and finally became a true Buddhist practitioner.

Everything in the mundane world has good and bad, large and small. For example, in giving charity, the more the charity, the greater the merit; the less the charity, the less the merit. Therefore, all things have differentiation. In the cultivation of the body, there is no killing, no stealing, and no sexual misconduct. In the cultivation of speech, there is no lying, no flattery, no double-tongued speech, and no harsh words. In the cultivation of the mind, there is no greed, no anger, and no wrong view. In the cultivation of body, speech, and mind, of course, each one is distinct. If we speak in terms of the true mind and intrinsic nature, they are originally pure and complete. Why then, do we need to cultivate and realize? How could there be diligence or neglect? Therefore, Chan Master Weikuan takes this as the heart of Chan.

金屑雖珍寶 在眼亦成病 见机当作者 善名是禅 八识心的禅

居白...

Like an Insect Eating Wood

One time, when Chan Master Guishan Lingyou was at the side of Chan Master Baizhang, Chan Master Baizhang asked, "Who's there?"

Chan Master Guishan replied, "Lingyou!"

Chan Master Baizhang said, "Poke around in the firepot and see if there is still a fire or not."

Chan Master Guishan stirred the ashes in the firepot and answered, "No fire."

Chan Master Baizhang stood up, went to the firepot, and used a poker to stir deeply in the firepot, causing a few sparks. He took out an ember to show to Guishan. Then he said, "You said there wasn't. Isn't this fire?"

Chan Master Guishan Lingyou said, "I know there is. It's just that I didn't poke deeply enough."

Chan Master Baizhang said, "This is just a temporary path off the main road. In the sutras, it says if you want to awaken to Buddha nature, you should contemplate timing, causes, and conditions. When the time and conditions come, it is like suddenly awakening from delusion, like suddenly remembering what was forgotten. Only then will you know that the self is originally complete; it is not obtained from outside. Therefore, the patriarch said,

> The awakened state is the same as non-awakening,
> No-mind is like mind.
> The ordinary and the sacred are illusory,
> Originally, the essence of the Dharma
> Is complete in and of itself.

"Right now, you are already like this. Carefully protect and hold onto it!"

The next day, Chan Master Guishan followed Chan Master Baizhang into the mountains to work. Chan Master Baizhang asked Guishan, "Did you bring the kindling?"

Chan Master Guishan answered, "I brought it."

Chan Master Baizhang pressed further, asking, "Where is it?"

Chan Master Guishan picked up a twig, blew on it twice, and then handed it to Chan Master Baizhang.

Chan Master Baizhang said happily, "Like an insect eating wood, occasionally a word is made."[75]

"Kindling"–what does it represent? What does it suggest? It is Buddha nature. When Chan Master Baizhang wanted Guishan to go to the firepot and stir the fire, this was hinting for him to find his own Buddha nature. Finding one's Buddha nature and the original mind is by no means easy. Chan Master Baizhang had no choice but to show him by example. Only by poking deeply can our intrinsic nature be revealed. Even when master and disciple went out to work, they were encouraging each other not to forget their intrinsic nature in daily life. In this phrase, "Did you bring the kindling," how much compassion, how much wisdom, how much living Chan there is.

聖心法原自備足
如虫禦木偶爾成文

《如虫禦木禾》
溈山靈佑曰
百文懷海

Is It Crooked? Is It Upright?

While Chan Master Jianyuan Zhongxing was the attendant of Chan Master Daowu, he was once serving tea to him when Chan Master Daowu pointed to the teacup and said, "Is it crooked? Is it upright?"

Zhongxing moved closer to Chan Master Daowu and faced him without saying a word. Chan Master Daowu said, "What is crooked will always be crooked; what is upright will always be upright."

Zhongxing shook his head and expressed his opinion, "I don't think so."

Daowu immediately asked, "Then, what is your view?"

Zhongxing snatched the teacup from Daowu's hand and held it in his own, loudly retorting, "Is it crooked? Is it upright?"

Daowu applauded and laughed loudly, saying, "No wonder you're my attendant."

Zhongxing then bowed to Chan Master Daowu.

The truth in Chan Master Daowu's instruction, "Is it upright? Is it crooked?" is that which we call, "When an evil person speaks the right teachings, the right teachings are also evil. When an upright person speaks the wrong teachings, the wrong teachings also become upright." Some people who speak daily of the Way, in fact, destroy people's faith. Some people who love to strike and like to scold can actually help people enter the Way. Great doctors, when treating illnesses, can turn arsenic and poison into good medicines. Therefore, we say, "What is evil will always be evil; what is upright will always be upright."

Chan Master Zhongxing believed that in the universe, "all dharmas arise due to conditions and all dharmas are extinguished due to conditions." When we can realize this, we will not attach to annihilation and eternity. When we come to this understanding, then everything is upright. If we are attached to whether the object in our hands has existence or is empty, then it is all evil. With this understanding, he turned the question on his teacher. Chan Master Daowu was gratified and praised him. Finally, the masters were harmonious in mind.

Can't Tell You

There was a student monk who wanted to go to the place where Chan Master Fuchuan resided. On the way, he happened to encounter an old man who sold salt, so he went up and asked him, "May I ask, old man, how do I get to the road to Fuchuan?"[76]

For a very long time, he waited without getting an answer from the old man so the student monk asked one more time.

The old man answered, "I've already told you. Are you deaf?"

The student monk replied, "What did you answer me with?"

The old man said, "I told you the road to Fuchuan."

The student monk asked, "Could it be that you also study Chan?"

The old man replied, "Not only Chan. I even know all of the Dharma."

The student monk said, "Then why don't you try saying it and let's see."

Without even saying a word, the old man shouldered his baskets of salt and was about to leave.

The student monk did not understand, only saying, "Difficult!"

The old man asked, "Why do you say that?"

The student monk said, "Old salt man!"

The old man responded, "Any instructions?"

The student monk asked, "What are you called?"

The old man replied, "I can't tell you this is salt."

To go to Chan Master Fuchuan's place to study, what road should we take? "Since it is said to be a capsized boat, how can there be a passageway?" The way has difficult paths and easy paths, the Mahayana path and Hinayana path, and the transcendent path and mundane path. The average student should always follow a path to make progress, but the student of the Chan School is like "the true man who has the will to charge heaven and not walk the path of the Tathagata." Even though it is a capsized boat, how can there not be a path?

丈夫自有衝天志
不向如來行處行

《不二文向你說》

藍帽宗學僧
霞復船語

Drying Mushrooms

In Eihei Temple,[77] there was a hunchbacked old Zen master in his eighties who was drying mushrooms under the hot sun. After the abbot, Zen Master Eihei Dogen, saw this he could not help but say, "Elder, you are so old. Why are you still exhausting yourself doing this kind of toilsome work? Please elder, you do not need to work so hard! I can find someone to do it for you!"

The old Zen master responded without any hesitation, "Other people are not me."

Eihei Dogen said, "That's true! However, if you want to work, you don't need to pick the hottest time of the day."

The old Zen Master replied, "If I don't dry mushrooms on a sunny day, do you mean to say I should wait to dry them on a cloudy or rainy day?"

Zen Master Eihei Dogen was the head of the temple and guided everyone. But when he encountered this old Zen master, he finally had to concede defeat.

In the Chan practitioners' life, no matter what the situation, they would not have someone else do the work, nor wait until tomorrow to do it. "Other people are not me" and "If I don't do it now, then when?" are issues that contemporary people should contemplate.

不經一翻寒徹骨
怎得梅花撲鼻香
直饒超佛不人流
荷地菩薩也算此方

老祖師馬道一禪師

Fly Beyond Birth and Death

There was a student monk named Daoxiu who although being skilled in Chan cultivation had never been able to awaken. He saw that of the fellow practitioners who had started practicing Chan and studying the Way later than him, quite a few were able to have some understanding of Chan. He thought about it and felt that he really had no qualifications for studying Chan–he was humorless and unclever–he had never been able to enter the Chan gate. He thought he might as well become a wandering ascetic monk. Therefore, Daoxiu packed his belongings of two-and-a-half catties,[78] planning to go far away. Right before he left, he went to the Dharma Hall to bid farewell to Chan Master Guangyu.

Daoxiu reported, "Teacher, your student does not live up to your compassion. It has already been ten years since I began studying under you, and I still don't have any insight into Chan. I'm really not someone with the potential for studying Chan. Today, I take my leave of you. I'll be traveling to other places."

Extremely surprised, Chan Master Guangyu asked, "Oh? Why are you leaving before you've had an awakening? Do you mean to say that by going somewhere else, you can attain awakening?"

Daoxiu earnestly reported again, "Every day, aside from eating and sleeping, I diligently focus on the cultivation of the Way. I work so hard, but the causes and conditions are not right. On the contrary, I see my Dharma brothers, one by one, returning to the origin with the right conditions. Now, in the depths of my heart, there grows a feeling of exhaustion. I think I'm better off being a wandering ascetic monk!"

After listening to this, Chan Master Guangyu instructed, "'Awakening' is a kind of manifestation of inner original nature. There is absolutely no way to describe it and it cannot be transmitted to other people. Furthermore, it cannot be learned or hurried. Other people's states are other people's; you cultivate your Chan Way. These are two different things. Why are you mixing them up?"

Daoxiu said, "Teacher, you don't understand! When I compare myself to my fellow practitioners, there is immediately the shame of being the small sparrow next to the Great Peng."[79]

Chan Master Guangyu, pretending as though he did not understand, asked, "How great is it? How small is it?"

Daoxiu said, "The Great Peng, with the spreading of its wings, can fly over hundreds of miles, yet I am confined to the area of a few feet on the grass."

Chan Master Guangyu meaningfully asked, "The Great Peng, with the spreading of its wings, can fly over hundreds of miles, but has it already flown beyond birth and death?"

After hearing this, Chan Monk Daoxiu was silent and did not speak, as though he had an awakening.

As the saying goes, "If people compare with others, they will be frustrated to death." Comparing and haggling are sources of affliction. How can we awaken to the Way through Chan then? Sharp and quick, the Great Peng can travel thousands of miles with the spreading of its wings, but it cannot fly beyond the great ocean of birth and death. Comparatively speaking, between the small sparrow and the Great Peng, there is fast and slow, tardy and quick; but Chan must flow from the equanimous intrinsic nature. Therefore, once the Chan monk Daoxiu eliminated his comparing and haggling and returned to his equanimous intrinsic nature, he was able to awaken.

佛在靈山莫遠求　靈山只在汝心頭
人人有個靈山塔　好向靈山塔下修

「免越生死」

道參廣圖

Not Permitted to be a Teacher

Chan Master Doushuai Congyue went to practice and study with the esoteric Chan Master Qingsu and was extremely respectful towards him. Once, because he was eating lychees, when he passed by Chan Master Qingsu's window, he very deferentially said, "Elder, this is fruit from my home province of Jiangxi. Please have some!"

Qingsu very joyfully accepted the lychees and said with a sigh, "Ever since my teacher passed away, I haven't had this fruit. It's been a long time."

Congyue asked, "Elder, which great master was your late teacher?"

Qingsu replied, "Chan Master Ciming. I served under him for thirteen years."

Extremely surprised, Chan Master Congyue said in admiration, "Having endured thirteen years of serving under him, you must have attained his Way!" As saying this, he offered all the lychees in his hands to Elder Qingsu.

Qingsu then gratefully said, "Because my merit was lacking, my late teacher instructed that I was not permitted to transmit to other people. Now, seeing that you are so devout and on account of this connection of lychees, I will actually go against the instructions of my late master. Tell me what you have learned from your practice."

Chan Master Congyue related all that he had experienced.

Qingsu instructed him, saying, "The world has both Buddha and Mara. When, in the end, you let go, you must to be able to enter the Buddha's Way and not enter Mara's."

After Chan Master Congyue received his approval, Chan Master Qingsu cautioned, "Today, I've pointed it out for you, allowing you to attain great liberation. But you cannot say that you succeeded me! Zhenjing Kewen is your teacher."

"To learn the Buddha Way, first make connections with others."[80] There was a connection made through lychees; then he was able to awaken to the Way. "The Dharma is sought in respect." Through the respect Congyue had for his predecessors, he was able to attain the Way. People in ancient times never forgot the thoughtfulness of a meal. Like Chan Master Qingsu, for an offering of lychees, he was actually willing to point out the mind's eye. This is being grateful for having connections. "You cannot succeed me, but you can succeed Chan Master Zhenjing Kewen" demonstrates the support and trust between masters, and is also an instructive anecdote of the Chan School.

Not Even a Thread

Bhiksuni Xuanji[81] of Jingju Temple often meditated and practiced Chan in a small cave on Mt. Dari. One day, a thought suddenly arose: "Dharma nature is pure and profound. It originally has no form of coming and going. Detesting noise and tending towards the tranquility of samadhi as I do, I cannot be considered a person who fully comprehends Dharma nature."

Therefore, she immediately set off to call upon Chan Master Xuefeng.[82]

When they first met, Xuefeng asked, "Where are you from?"

Xuanji replied, "Mt. Dari."

Using sharp words, Xuefeng asked, "Has the sun come out yet or not?"

Xuanji, unwilling to show weakness, said, "If the sun comes out, it will melt the snowy peak."

Xuefeng saw that her response was out of the ordinary. He then asked, "What is your name?"

"Xuanji."

"How much can you weave in a day?"

"Not even a thread!"[83]

When Xuanji had bowed and was withdrawing, just as she had taken just a few steps, Xuefeng said, "Your robe is dragging on the ground!"

After Xuanji heard this, she quickly turned her head and glanced at the hem of her robe. Xuefeng roared with laughter and said, "Some 'not even a thread' you are!"

From the exchange between Xuanji and Xuefeng, we see the different states of Chan. Xuanji's words were quick and sharp–they were not Chan. Chan Master Xuefeng's one line, "Some 'not even a thread' you are!"–now that is the spirit of Chan.

妙性深湛
本來妙
去之相
意樣
雪外
鐵橛子
對個寸
掛絲
不掛寸絲
注雪機峰

Wild Fox Chan

Chan Master Baizhang Huaihai was Chan Master Mazu Daoyi's successor. From "Mazu founded the Chinese monastic community, Baizhang established the monastic regulations," we can see his contribution to the Chan School.

One day, after Chan Master Baizhang had completed his talk on the Dharma and everyone had already departed, an old man stayed and did not go. The Chan Master asked, "Who is standing before me?"

The old man replied, "I am not a human being. Actually, I am a wild fox.[84] In the time of the ancient Buddhas, I practiced on this very Mt. Baizhang. Later, a student monk asked me, 'Do great practitioners still fall under cause and effect, or not?' and I answered, 'They don't fall under cause and effect!' Because of this one answer, I've been reborn in the body of a fox for five hundred lifetimes. Today, I ask the Chan Master to help me with a turning word so that I may be liberated from the wild fox's form."

After Chan Master Baizhang heard this, he said compassionately, "Please ask."

The old man joined palms and asked, "Do great practitioners still fall under cause and effect, or not?"

Chan Master Baizhang replied, "They're not ignorant[85] of cause and effect."

With these words, the old man had a great awakening. Afterwards, he made a bow and took his leave. The next day, Chan Master Baizhang led everyone in the monastery to a cave in the mountain behind the monastery, where he pulled out the dead body of a wild fox with his staff. The Chan Master instructed that it be cremated in accordance with the rites of a deceased monastic.

This is a famous gongan. Why was he reborn in the body of a fox for five hundred lifetimes just because he answered the student monk by saying, "They don't fall under cause and effect"? Why was he able to be liberated from the suffering of five hundred lifetimes in the body of a fox when Chan Master Baizhang said a turning word, "They're not ignorant of cause and effect," on his behalf? Between them, there is the difference of a few words; but actually, there is a difference of heaven and earth. The question was: "Do great practitioners still fall under cause and effect, or not?" The answer said: "They do not fall under cause and effect." This suggests that people with cultivation are not affected by the retribution of cause and effect. This kind of careless and reckless instruction is mistaken, because no one can escape from the retribution of cause and effect. Chan Master Baizhang's "They're not ignorant of cause and effect" is actually a saying of the supreme truth because anyone who has cultivated and awakened to the Way must not be "ignorant of cause and effect."

Therefore, Chan Master Wumen once had a verse that said:

Not falling, not ignorant,
Two banners in competition[86]
Not ignorant, not falling,
A thousand mistakes, ten thousand mistakes.

野狐禪

百丈懷海示野狐

Reform the Self

Zen Master Ryokan cultivated and practiced Chan his entire life, never wasting a single day. When he was old, news came from his hometown that his nephew was not engaged in any legitimate profession but was gambling, eating, playing around, and on the verge of squandering the family's wealth. The elders of his hometown hoped this Zen master uncle could show great compassion and save his nephew by urging him to repent and turn over a new leaf.

In the end, because Zen Master Ryokan was moved by affection for his hometown, he made light of the hardship and walked for three days, returning to his childhood home. Zen Master Ryokan finally met the nephew whom he had not seen in many years. This nephew was very happy to be reunited with his monastic uncle and expressly asked him to stay for the night.

Zen Master Ryokan spent the night on the bed in his family's home in sitting meditation. The next morning, when he was leaving, he said to his nephew, "I suppose I really am getting old—my two hands are constantly trembling. Can you please help me tie the laces of my straw sandals?"

His nephew was more than happy to lend a hand. Zen Master Ryokan said kindly, "Thank you. You see, when people get old, they decline day by day. You have to take good care of yourself. While you're young, you should be a good person and lay the foundation for your career."

After the Zen Master finished speaking, he turned and left. With regard to any of his nephew's unwholesome behavior, he did not mention a word. However, from that day forth, his nephew no longer led a life of debauchery.

The teaching method of Chan sometimes stuns with a blow or a shout; sometimes refutes by questioning insistently; sometimes does not determine having and not having; and sometimes hints at implied meanings. In short, Chan education does not directly point things out. Only that which is not directly pointed out to us is completely our own.

To all parents who love and care about your children: Can you understand this kind of Chan mind?

这于治
迷儿
老归家
智见凄心
良宽
少惜丁
住勤
帮履
不远往
更以人
去年
出远图本以
良宽
京场

-175-

I Don't Know

During the Song Dynasty, there was a General Cao Han. After subduing bandits and rebels in the South, he passed by Yuantong Monastery on Mt. Lu. The monastics of the temple, because they knew that Cao Han's army was poorly disciplined, all fearfully scattered in the four directions to get away. Only the abbot, Chan Master Yuande, sat meditating in the Dharma Hall without moving. Cao Han called out to him, but the Chan Master ignored him, unwilling to even give him a glance. Cao Han's heroic pride suffered a blow and he very angrily said, "My army was passing through this place and only wanted to stay overnight at your temple to allow the soldiers to rest a while. Why haven't you offered even a word of welcome? How dare you be so unreasonable! Don't you know that standing before you is a general who kills without batting an eye?"

After the Chan Master heard this, he calmly opened his eyes and responded, "A soldier standing before the Buddha roaring with rage. This is so disrespectful. Aren't you afraid of karmic retribution?"

Cao Han roared even louder, "What karmic retribution! Aren't you afraid to die?"

Chan Master Yuande also raised his voice, saying, "Don't you know that sitting before you is a Chan monk who isn't afraid to die?"

Cao Han was really astonished at the Chan Master's courage. At the same time, he was also brought into submission by the Chan Master's samadhi. He asked, "Such a large monastery, yet only you remain. Where are the others?"

Chan Master Yuande said, "You just have to strike the drum. They will hear the sound and return."

Cao Han then forcefully beat the drum. He beat it for a long time, but still, no one appeared. Displeased, Cao Han said, "I've already beaten the drum. Why hasn't anyone returned yet?"

Chan Master Yuande calmly said, "That's because, when you beat the drum, your murderous aura was too strong. Please recite 'Namo Sakyamuni Buddha' once, and then beat it one time."

Therefore, Cao Han recited the Buddha's name and beat the drum, beat the drum and recited the Buddha's name. Before long, the monks of the monastery who were hiding all came running back. At this time, Cao Han very respectfully joined palms and asked, "May I inquire as to the Chan Master's Dharma name?"

The Chan Master serenely replied, "I am Yuande."

Cao Han was completely in awe. Immediately falling to his knees, he implored, "So all along it was the virtuous and noble Chan Master Yuande! Chan Master, please instruct me: how can I be victorious in battle?"

Chan Master Yuande coolly answered, "I don't know."

Since ancient times, whenever society has experienced war there were always some great sages who protected the temples, willing to live or die with them. Those like Chan Master Yuande were people of courage, compassion, and wisdom. Not fleeing from disasters of military action is courage, telling people to recite the Buddha's name is compassion, and answering according to conditions is wisdom. In particular, one who answers the question of how to achieve victory in battle with "I don't know" truly is a great sage with wisdom, compassion, and courage. Is this not the function of the Chan mind?

人生．此處
知何州
應已死
隨路雪
況之上
偶留指
爪印
鴻飛
那後計
東西
《示達》
緣隨
弘豐稿

The Whole Body Is the Eye

One time, Chan Master Daowu asked Yunyan, "Avalokitesvara Bodhisattva has a thousand hands and a thousand eyes. May I ask you, which eye is the true eye?"

Yunyan replied, "It's like when you're sleeping at night and the pillow falls onto the ground. Without opening your eyes, your hand reaches to the floor for it and immediately picks it up. Then you go back to sleep. Let me ask you: which eye did you use to pick it up?"

After Chan Master Daowu heard this, he said, "Oh! Dharma brother, now I understand."

"What do you understand?"

"All over the body is the eye."

Chan Master Yunyan smiled and said, "You only understand eighty percent."

Confused, Daowu asked, "Then, what should I say?"

"The whole body is the eye."

"All over the body is the eye"–this is recognizing through discriminating consciousness. "The whole body is the eye"–this is revealing non-discriminating wisdom from the nature of the mind. We have a true mind in which the entire body is the eye, so why not use it to completely contemplate and illuminate everything?

観
世
音
菩
薩
千
手
千
眼

通
身
是
眼

眼
睛
去
了
间

《通
身
是
眼》

雪
岩
悟
道
紫
小
道

The Way of Nurturing Talent

After paying respect to the Buddha in the Buddha Hall, a devotee then wandered into the garden for a stroll and happened to see the head gardener[87] busily tending to the flowers and plants. He just saw him with a pair of shears rising and falling in his hands, cutting off branches and leaves, uprooting plants and transplanting them to another pot, or watering and fertilizing some withered branches, giving them special care. Not understanding, the devotee asked, "Head Gardening Chan Master, when taking care of plants, why do you cut off the healthy branches and leaves? Why do you water and fertilize the withered branches and trunks instead? Furthermore, why move one pot to another and why is it necessary to hoe the land where there are no plants at all? Do you need to go to such trouble?"

The head gardening Chan master said, "Taking care of plants is exactly like educating your children. However we educate people, the same goes for plants."

After the devotee heard this, taking exception, he said, "Flowers, grasses, and trees–how can you compare them with people?"

The head gardening Chan master said without raising his head, "When caring for plants, first, with regard to those plants that appear to be lush and flourishing but are actually growing wildly and unruly, you must get rid of the branches and knots and pluck away the wayward leaves, so as not to waste nutrients. In the future, they will then be able to grow well. This is like reining in the arrogance of young people, eliminating their bad habits, and putting them on the right track. Second, uproot the plant and move it to another pot. The purpose is to separate the plant from barren soil and put it in contact with fertile soil. This is like removing young people from a bad environment to another place to meet good teachers and helpful friends, so that they may gain greater knowledge. Third, especially water the withered branches, because, in reality, the withered branches of those plants that appear to be dead contain within them unlimited vitality. Do not think that bad children all cannot be saved, get discouraged with them, and give up. You should know that human nature is originally good. As long as we wholeheartedly love and care for them in the right way, we can ultimately give them a new life. Fourth, till the fallow ground, because actually, in the earth there are seeds waiting to sprout. This is like those students who are poor but have the mind to strive for the better; we help them, allowing them to have new opportunities to grow strong."

After the devotee heard this, he very joyfully said, "Head Gardening Chan Master, thank you for giving me a lesson on the way of nurturing talent."

The Nirvana Sutra *says, "Sentient and non-sentient beings have the same perfect wisdom." In the world, there is no life we cannot save, no person we cannot educate. At the front gate of the monastery, there is usually a statue of a smiling Maitreya Bodhisattva. Its significance is to use compassion (love) to draw us in. But behind Maitreya Bodhisattva stands the statue of General Skanda, demon-conquering staff in hand. Its significance is to use force (strength) to subdue us. When parents and teachers give young people both love to reach them and strength to subdue them, these children cannot but become useful people!*

全生的堪
發力的
坊眼
情六世情
閒圖
智種

「育才之道」
園頭對信徒

Everything Is Chan

A wandering monk heard others say that Chan Master Wuxiang's cultivation of Chan was excellent, so he wanted to debate with him about the methods of Chan. It just so happened that the Chan Master was away, and the attendant novice monk came out to receive the visitor, saying, "The Chan Master isn't here. If you need something, I can help you in his place."

The wandering monk said, "You're too young. You can't."

The novice attendant replied, "Although my age is young, my wisdom is not insignificant!"

As soon as the wandering monk heard this, he felt it wasn't too bad. He then drew a small circle with his finger and pointed ahead. The attendant spread out both of his hands and drew a big circle. The wandering monk held out a finger. The attendant held out five fingers. The wandering monk then held out three fingers. The attendant pointed at his eyes with his hand.

Very uneasy and afraid, the wandering monk knelt down, prostrated three times, turned around, and left. The wandering monk thought to himself, "I drew a small circle with my hand and pointed ahead to ask him, 'How great is your capacity?' He spread out both hands and drew a big circle, saying it was as big as the ocean. I then held out one finger to ask him, 'How about yourself?' He held out five fingers, saying that he upholds the Five Precepts. I then held out three fingers to ask him, 'How about the three realms?' He pointed at his eyes, saying that the three realms are within the eyes. If even the attendant is this wise, then who knows how deep the cultivation of Chan Master Wuxiang is! I think my best course of action is to leave."

Later, when Chan Master Wuxiang returned, the attendant reported all that had happened, saying, "Master, I don't know why that wandering monk knew my family sells cakes. He drew a small circle with his hands, saying, 'Your family's cakes are only this big.' I then spread out both hands to say, 'They are this big.' He held out one finger, saying, 'One for one penny?' I held out five fingers to say, 'Five pennies will buy you one.' He then held out three fingers, saying, 'Will three pennies do?' I thought, 'Too heartless!' and pointed at my eyes, accusing him of not knowing their value. I never thought he would run away in fear!"

After Chan Master Wuxiang heard this, he said, "Everything is Dharma; everything is Chan! Attendant, do you understand?"

The attendant was at a loss and did not know how to respond.

Buddhist teaching stresses the right conditions. Chan is the right conditions. If you understand this, there is no moment that is not Chan, no place that is not Chan, no person that is not Chan, nothing that is not Chan. If you do not understand this, even if it is said in a flowery way, it has nothing to do with Chan. In the history of Chan, there are the tales of Zhaozhou's tea and Yunmen's cakes.[88] They are all Chan. There is a saying, "The speaker has no intent, but the listener has his own notions." Therefore, Chan Master Wuxiang said, "Everything is Dharma; everything is Chan."

当时大禅名庆不谙
无人心禅无事不禅

《一切皆禅》当相示侍者

Cutting Off Ears to Save the Pheasant

Chan Master Zhishun of the Tang Dynasty had always traveled far and wide to practice Chan. One day, while sitting in meditation in a mountain forest, he suddenly saw a hunter shoot a pheasant. The wounded pheasant fled to where the Chan Master was seated. The Chan Master used the sleeves of his robe to conceal this little creature that had narrowly escaped danger. Shortly afterwards, the hunter ran up to the Chan Master and demanded the pheasant, "Please give me back that pheasant I shot!"

The Chan Master, with patience and infinite compassion, explained to the hunter, "It is also a living being. Spare it!"

"You should know, that pheasant could be a meal for me!"

The hunter continued to pester the Chan Master. There was nothing the Chan Master could do, so he immediately picked up the knife he used for self-defense when traveling, cut off his own ears, gave them to the greedy hunter, and said, "These two ears, are they enough to make up for your pheasant? You can take them to make your meal."

The hunter was really shocked and finally realized that hunting to kill is the height of cruelty.

For the sake of saving and protecting living beings, one does not hesitate to sacrifice one's own body. The virtue of "For the sake of helping sentient beings attain liberation from suffering, do not seek tranquility and happiness for oneself" is precisely the concrete manifestation of the Chan Master's compassion. Chan practitioners do not avoid society nor do they distance themselves from people. The eager actions of Chan practitioners in forsaking self to save others can be seen in Chan Master Zhishun's cutting off his ears to save the pheasant.

願眾生得離苦不為自己求安樂

今割耳牧雞
智舞畫猴人

One and Two

In the history of Chinese Buddhism, Daoist priests and Buddhist monastics have often debated and fought over truth.

A Daoist priest once said to Chan Master Fayin, "No matter what, your Buddhism cannot compare with our Daoism because Buddhism's highest realm is 'one mind,' is 'One Vehicle,' is 'one true dharma realm.' 'One Buddha, one Tathagata' are also 'one.' But whatever our Daoism speaks of is always in terms of 'two.' We can say that 'two' surpasses your 'one.' For instance, 'heaven and earth,'[89] 'Yin and Yang'; these are all 'two.' Actually, 'two' is superior to your 'one'."

After Chan Master Fayin heard this, appearing not to understand, he asked, "Really? Can your 'two' really surpass our 'one'?"

The Daoist priest said, "So long as you say 'one,' I can say 'two.' I would certainly be able to surpass you.

Chan Master Fayin then lifted up a leg and slowly said, "I have now raised one leg. Can you lift up both your legs?"

The Daoist priest was rendered speechless!

In the history of Buddhism, there are records of four imperial persecutions[90] of the religion in China, most of which were caused by the envy and hatred of Daoist priests towards Buddhism. In the West, there was the struggle between Catholicism and Protestantism. In India, there were clashes between Hinduism and Islam. Buddhism advocates peace, but it was still difficult to avoid disharmony with Daoism. Even "one and two" became a subject of debate, just like Chan Master Fayin's means of skillful debate is also an ingenious application of Chan.

百千法門同歸
方寸，河沙妙德、總在心源

《一占二》法印勤道士

Honesty without Deception

After Chan Master Daokai of the Song Dynasty had attained the Way, he expounded on the style of Chan practice. He had served as the abbot of big temples such as Jingyin Temple and Tianning Temple. One day, the emperor[91] dispatched an envoy to bestow a purple kasaya in praise of his sagely virtue and confer upon him the title of "Chan Master Dingzhao–Samadhi Illumination."

The Chan Master resolutely declined to accept. The emperor then ordered Li Xiaoshou, a member of the imperial family in Kaifeng, to go to the Chan Master to convey the imperial court's commendations and good intentions. The Chan Master still would not accept. As a result, the emperor was infuriated and issued an imperial decree for the prefect to take him into custody. The prefect knew that the Chan Master was benevolent, generous, loyal, and honest. When he arrived at the temple, he quietly asked, "The Chan Master's body is weak and his face looks haggard. Are you ill?"

The Chan Master replied, "No!"

The prefect said, "If you say you're sick, then you can avoid punishment for defying the imperial decree."

The Chan Master said, "If I'm not sick, then I'm not sick. How could I feign illness in order to avoid punishment?"

The prefect had no choice but to banish the Chan Master to Zizhou. All those who heard about it wept without end.

We often see that the personalities of Chan practitioners are witty and lively. However, the honesty and persistence of Chan practitioners can be seen in Chan Master Daokai's conduct and virtue. As Venerable Master Lianchi of the Ming Dynasty[92] said in praise, "When honor comes, to decline it is difficult for people. To decline and bring about punishment, and to receive punishment but not deceive–is this not the most difficult of difficulties? In the biographies of the loyal and righteous, how could this be left out? I record it as a model for the monastics of the world."

A Taste of Chan

During the Tang Dynasty, there was a Chan Master Lanzan who lived in seclusion in a cave on Mt. Nanyue in Hunan Province. He once wrote a poem expressing his state of mind:

Worldly affairs pass slowly by,
Incomparable to the mountains and hills,
Lying under wisteria vines,
With a stone for my pillow.
No audience with the Son of Heaven,
Why envy princes and nobles?
No worries about life and death,
What further distress could there be?

The meaning of this poem explained his carefree life. Afterwards, when the poem reached the ears of the Tang Emperor Dezong, Dezong very much wanted to meet this Chan Master and see what kind of person he was. Therefore, he dispatched an official to welcome the Chan Master to the imperial court.

The official, carrying the imperial decree, found the cave just in time to see the Chan Master cooking inside the cave. At the mouth of the cave, the official then cried out loudly, "The imperial decree has arrived. Quick! Kneel down to receive it!" Inside the cave, Chan Master Lanzan, pretending to be deaf and dumb, did not pay him the slightest bit of attention.

The official poked his head in and only saw the Chan Master using cow dung to stoke the fire. Roasting in a clay pot were sweet potatoes. The fire burned more and more intensely, smoke permeated everywhere, and black fog swirled around and around completely engulfing the inside and outside of the cave. Smoke assailed the Chan Master, causing tears and mucus to run down his face. Seeing this, the attending guard could not help but call out, "Hey Chan Master! Snot is dripping down your nose! Why don't you wipe it off?"

Chan Master Lanzan, without even turning his head, replied, "I don't have the time to clean off snot for ordinary people!"

After Chan Master Lanzan said this, he immediately picked up a piping hot sweet potato, put it in his mouth, and said again and again in praise, "Delicious! Delicious!"

Seeing this, the official was stunned speechless because what Chan Master Lanzan was actually eating was one rock after another. While Chan Master Lanzan was eating, he casually picked up two more and handed them to the official, saying, "Please eat them while they're hot! The three realms are only of the mind; the myriad dharmas are only of the consciousness. Poor and rich, noble and mean, raw and cooked, soft and hard–in the ground of the mind and the ocean of consciousness, do not separate them into two."

The official, seeing the Chan Master's unusual behavior and hearing his inscrutable Dharma teaching, did not dare answer, so he hurried back to the imperial court and faithfully reported to the emperor. After listening to this, Emperor Dezong sighed with great emotion and said, "That our country has such a Chan master is truly everyone's blessing!"

Among monastics, there are bhiksus of the people and there are also bhiksus who live in seclusion. The bhiksus of the people propagate the Dharma to benefit sentient beings and serve society. The bhiksus living in seclusion in caves deep in the mountains tranquilly cultivate the Way. Some bhiksus living among people are in the mundane world, but their minds are in the mountain forests. Some bhiksus living in seclusion are in a place of practice, but their minds are in the secular world. Like Chan Master Lanzan, when he met with the favor of the emperor, he looked upon it as a summons from Yama, the King of Hell; when rewarded with treasures, he regarded them as burdens. He truly is a sagely monastic who transcended the human world.

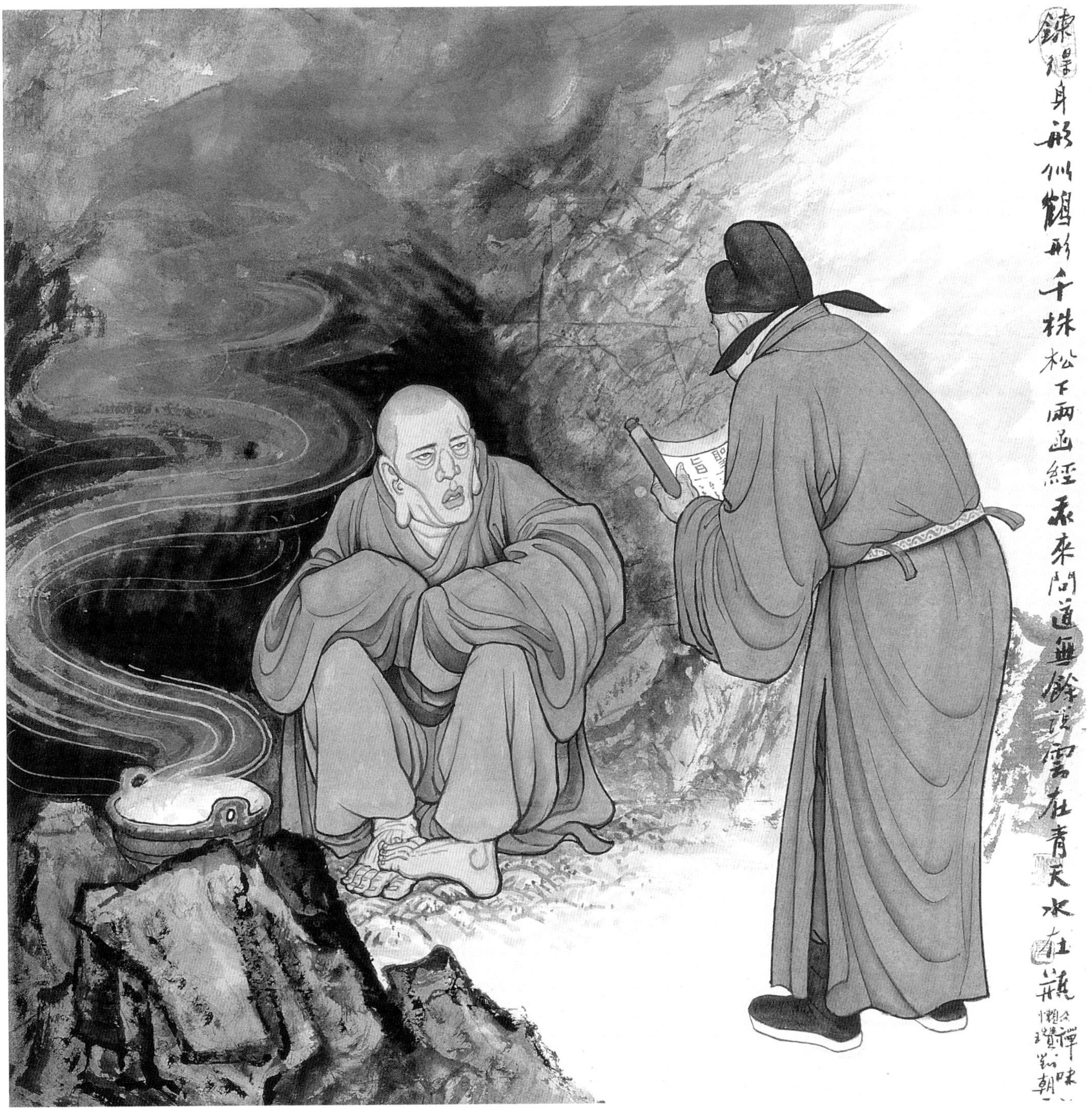
鍊得身形似鶴形千株松下兩函經我來問道無餘說雲在青天水在瓶

Transferring Merits

There was a farmer who respectfully invited Chan Master Wuxiang to his home to recite sutras for his deceased wife. After the Dharma service had ended, the farmer asked, "Chan Master, how much benefit do you think my wife can receive from this Dharma service?"

Chan Master Wuxiang truthfully said, "Of course! The Dharma is like a boat of compassion that ferries all beings to liberation, or like sunlight that shines everywhere. Not only can your wife receive benefit, but all sentient beings, without exception, will receive benefit."

Unsatisfied, the farmer said, "But my wife was very delicate and frail. Other sentient beings may take advantage of her and rob her of her merit. Could you recite the sutras for her alone, and not transfer the merit to other sentient beings?"

Chan Master Wuxiang sighed at the farmer's selfishness, but he still compassionately explained, "Transferring one's own merit to others, so that every sentient being equally shares in the benefits of the Dharma is a very good Dharma method of cultivation. The meaning of "transferring merits" includes returning the phenomena to the principle, returning the causes to the effects, and returning the small to the big. Just like a light does not shine on one person; a light can shine on all people. Just like the one sun in the sky envelopes all things in its illumination, one seed can produce thousands of fruit. You should use the candle lit by your heart to light millions of other candles. Not only does the brightness increase by a million fold, but your own candle also does not diminish in radiance because of this. If everyone could embrace this concept, then our diminutive self would receive much benefit because of the transferring of merit by innumerable people. Why not do it happily then? Therefore, we Buddhists practitioners should treat all sentient beings equally!"

The farmer still stubbornly said, "This teaching is very good, but I still want to ask the Master to make an exception. I have a neighbor, Old Zhao. It could be said that he bullies me and entraps me. If I could just exclude him from 'all sentient beings,' that would be great."

Chan Master Wuxiang said in a stern tone, "Since I said everything, how could there be exceptions?"

The farmer was completely at a loss.

In this person of the farmer, we can completely see the selfishness, pettiness, and narrow-mindedness of human nature. As long as he is happy and has what he desires, who cares whether other people are dead or alive. How could you not know that other people are suffering, and indulge yourself? Speaking in terms of the world, there are the two aspects of phenomena and principle. With regard to the forms of phenomena, there are variations in number and there are differences. However, with regard to the principle, there is no variation in number and there are no differences. Everything is equal. This is the same as a lamp illuminating a dark room—the entire room is bright. How could it just shine on one object, other objects not benefiting from the light?

Only those who understand everything can embrace everything. To abandon one is to abandon all. If you abandon everything, what else is there in life?

事回理向小問大如燈些定些光明通徹無相妙法身一合相向無句

Purify the Mind, Purify the Land

There was a devout Buddhist devotee who picked fresh flowers from her own garden every day and brought them to the temple to make an offering to the Buddha. One day, just as she was delivering flowers to the Buddha Hall, she happened to run into Chan Master Wude who was coming out of the Dharma Hall. Chan Master Wude said joyfully, "You come so devoutly every day with fragrant flowers to make offerings to the Buddha! According to accounts in the sutras, those who often make offerings of fragrant flowers to the Buddha will have the blessing of a dignified countenance in a future life."

The devotee very happily replied, "This is as it should be. Every time I come to the temple to pay my respects to the Buddha, I feel that my spirit is pure and refreshed, as though it has been washed clean. But when I get home, my mind is troubled and agitated. As a housewife, how can I maintain a pure and clear mind in the chaotic and noisy city?"

Chan Master Wude asked in return, "Since you offer fresh flowers to the Buddha, I believe you must have some general knowledge regarding plants. I now ask you: how do you preserve the freshness of flowers?"

The devotee answered, "The way to preserve the freshness of flowers is nothing other than changing the water every day and, when changing the water, cutting off a section of the stem because the end of the stem in the water rots easily. After it rots, the moisture is difficult to absorb, so it withers easily!"

Chan Master Wude said, "To maintain a pure and clear mind, the principle is also the same. Our living environment is like the water in a vase and we are the flowers. Only by continuously purifying our bodies and minds, changing our dispositions, and constantly repenting, examining ourselves, and correcting our bad habits and faults, can we unceasingly absorb the nutrients from nature."

After the devotee heard this, she happily bowed and gratefully said, "Thank you, Chan Master, for your instruction. I hope, in the future, I'll have the opportunity to be near the Chan Master, to live the life of a Chan practitioner in the monastery, and to enjoy the tranquility of the morning bell, evening drum, and bodhi chanting."

Chan Master Wude said, "Your breathing is the chanting, the beating of your pulse is the bell and drum, your body is the temple, and your two ears are bodhi. There is no place that is not tranquil. Why must you wait for an opportunity to live in a monastery?"

An ancient virtuous one said, "Make the bustling marketplace a place of practice." Tranquility–so long as we cease our delusional conditions and cast aside distracting thoughts, where can there not be tranquility? Ancient monasteries deep in the mountains–if we do not rid ourselves of delusional thinking, even if we live in ancient monasteries deep in the mountains, we will still be unable to cultivate. Chan practitioners emphasize "the present moment." Why tomorrow? "When practicing Chan, what need is there for mountains, water, or land? But when you extinguish the fire of the mind, it is cool."[93] This is the way to describe it.

Salty and Plain Have Flavor

An artist who became a Buddhist, Master Hongyi combined Buddhist practice and the artistic life, which allowed us to more clearly see his state of life. One day, the renowned educator, Mr. Xia Mianzun, came to pay him a visit. When they were eating, Mr. Xia saw him eating only one dish of pickled vegetables and could not help but say, "You don't think those pickled vegetables are too salty?"

Master Hongyi answered, "Salty has its own flavor!"

Awhile later, after Master Hongyi had finished eating, he held a cup of boiled water in his hands. Furrowing his brow, Mr. Xia said, "No tea leaves? How can you drink that plain water every day?"

Master Hongyi then smiled and said, "Although boiled water is plain, plain also has its own flavor."

Master Hongyi's "Salty has its own flavor, plain has its own flavor" is a saying that is very rich in the flavor of the Dharma and Chan. Master Hongyi applied the Dharma to his daily life, so there was no place in his life that did not have flavor. A towel that had been used for three years and was already torn— he would say that it could still be used. Staying at an inn with bedbugs crawling here and there—the guests complained, but he would say that there were only a few. It can be said that he truly understood the life of "feeling at ease under all conditions."

That Is Chan

Kusuda was a skilled physician, but many of his patients still died. For this reason, he feared the shadow of death every day. Once, on the way to make a house call, he happened to meet a wandering monk. Kusuda then asked for instruction, saying, "What is Chan?"

The wandering monk answered, "I don't know how to tell you, but there is one thing I am certain of: once you understand Chan, you won't need to fear death." So, at the direction of the wandering monk, Kusuda went to seek instruction from Zen Master Nannin.

Doctor Kusuda found the residence of Zen Master Nannin, explained the purpose of his visit, and asked for instruction.

Zen Master Nannin said, "Chan is not hard to learn. Since you are a doctor, you should treat your patients carefully. That is Chan!"

Not quite understanding, Doctor Kusuda visited Zen Master Nannin three times altogether. Zen Master Nannin always said to him, "A doctor shouldn't while away his time every day in a monastery. Hurry home and take care of your patients!"

Extremely bewildered, Doctor Kusuda thought, "How can this kind of instruction get rid of the mind that fears death?" Therefore, when he went to visit a fourth time, he complained, "A wandering monk once told me that as soon as a person learns Chan, he will not fear death. Every time I come here, you always want me to take care of my patients. With regard to this point, I am very clear. However, if this is what is called Chan, in the future, I won't need to come again to seek instruction from you."

Zen Master Nannin smilingly patted Kusuda on the shoulder and said, "I've been too strict with you. Let me give you a gongan to try!"

The gongan that Zen Master Nannin wanted Kusuda to contemplate was the huatou of "Zhaozhou's *Wu*."[94] Kusuda diligently contemplated this gongan of the word "*wu*" for two years. When he told Zen Master Nannin of his state of mind, the answer he got was, "You have not yet entered the state of Chan!" Kusuda, not losing heart, remained single-minded and contemplated it for another year-and-a-half. Finally, he felt his mind-ground was clear and bright, and the difficult problem gradually disappeared. "*Wu*" had already become the truth. He gave his best treatment to his patients without knowing it. He had broken away from his anxiety over life and death.

In the end, when he called on Zen Master Nannin, the Zen Master merely smiled and said one thing: "From forgetting self to no-self, that is precisely the manifestation of Chan mind."

Doctor Kusuda frequently came into contact with people who were aging, ailing, dying, and being born. As a result, "When I see other people die, my mind is anxious like fire. I am not grieving for others; look, look, it is my turn." So, with regard to death, fear arises. Zen Master Nannin's wanting him to take good care of his patients is practicing Chan, because if someone abandons his responsibility and gives up his compassion, how can he enter Chan? When he had contemplated to the point of penetrating the "Wu" gongan, he went from mind to no-mind, from self to no-self, from birth to no-birth. That is the Chan state without death.

達摩西來一字無全憑心地用功夫若要紙上淡人我筆影醺乾洞庭湖〈那就是禪〉南陽示王田

True and False–Deluded Words

Chan Master Daoguang once asked Chan Master Dazhu Huihai, "Chan Master, usually, when you are diligently practicing, which mind do you use to cultivate the Way?"

Dazhu answered, "This old monk has no mind to use, no Way to cultivate."

Daoguang said, "Since there is no mind to use and no Way to cultivate, why do you gather a crowd every day, encouraging people to practice Chan and cultivate the Way?"

Dazhu then said, "This old monk has no roof tiles above and no ground to stand on below. How can there be a place for gathering people?"

Daoguang responded, "In fact, you gather people every day to discuss the Way. Is this not teaching the Dharma to liberate sentient beings?"

Dazhu said, "Please don't wrong me. I don't even know how to speak. How can I discuss the Way? I don't even see a single person. How can you say that I liberate sentient beings?"

Daoguang answered, "Chan Master, you speak deluded words."

Dazhu said, "This old monk doesn't even have a tongue. How can I say deluded words?"

Daoguang replied, "Is it possible that the physical world, the sentient world, the existence of you and me, and the reality of practicing Chan and teaching the Dharma are all false?"

Dazhu said, "They're all true!"

Daoguang asked, "Since they are true, why must you negate them all?"

Dazhu replied, "What is false must be negated; what is true must also be negated!"

Finally, with these words, Daoguang had a great awakening.

To speak of the truth, sometimes we recognize it from affirmation. However, other times, we can recognize it from negation. Like the Heart Sutra *says, "Form is emptiness, emptiness is form. Sensation, perception, mental formation, and consciousness are also like this." This is recognizing human life and the world from affirmation. The* Heart Sutra *also says, "No eyes, ears, nose, tongue, body, mind; no form, sound, smell, taste, touch, and dharmas." This is recognizing human life and the world from negation. Chan Master Dazhu Huihai's famous statement of negating everything is not deluded speech because only by negating everything can you affirm everything.*

Explanatory Notes

1. The *gongan* of Chan Master Nanquan killing a cat appears in the *Wumen Guan* (*Wumen's Gate*), case 14.

2. "Zen" is the Japanese word for the Chinese *Chan*. Since most of the masters in this book belong to the Chinese Chan tradition and Venerable Master Hsing Yun is of the Linji lineage, the term "Chan" is used instead of the more widely known "Zen." However, in the stories of Japanese masters, they are called by their Japanese title and name.

3. In Buddhism, the term "space" refers to that which has no limits or boundaries, is permanent and eternal, and embraces everything.

4. Daoism is a Chinese philosophical and religious system that was founded in sixth century B.C.E. by Laozi (604-531 B.C.E.). His teachings were passed down orally until they were compiled in a book called the *Dao De Jing* during the third century B.C.E.

5. The Chinese word for "change" and "conjure" is *bian*.

6. The Dharma has only one essence and is without any offshoots.

7. Chan practitioners would travel from temple to temple, studying with and visiting teachers of the Way. The term *canfang* literally means to "investigate" and "visit."

8. "Afflictions" are states of mind that cloud the mind's nature and lead to unwholesome actions of body, speech, and mind. It is also translated as "defilements" and "vexations."

9. The name "Heizhi" literally means "black finger."

10. "Special transmission outside the scriptures" refers to the Southern Chan School's teaching method, which does not rely on texts or writings but rather on mind-to-mind transmission.

11. In the *Wumen Guan*, case 28, Deshan encounters an old woman selling refreshments by the road. When he asks her if he could buy some, she says, "As it says in the *Diamond Sutra*, the past mind cannot be found, the present mind cannot be found, and the future mind cannot be found. What mind do you wish to refresh, Virtuous One?" He is unable to answer, and asks if there is a Chan master in the area. The old lady sends him to Longtan.

12. In Chinese, one *li* is a unit of measure about one-third of a mile. Five *li* would be approximately one-and-a-half miles.

13. The name "Longtan" means "dragon pond."

14. Deshan is referring to the teachings of all the Chan masters in the world.

15. Wumen's verse appears in the *Wumen Guan*, case 17.

16. A cangue is an implement of punishment and torture used in ancient China.

17. In Chinese, "Mt. Wutai" is known as "Wutai shan." The word *shan* means "mountain."

18. The reference to "three three in front, three three in back" appears in the *Blue Cliff Record*, case 35.

19. The Chinese word *xian*, translated here as "snubbed," can also mean "give the cold shoulder."

20. "It" refers to one's intrinsic nature.

21. The Hanlin Imperial Academy was founded during the Tang Dynasty. It was a government institution staffed with the best scholars who prepared official documents for the emperor.

22. In Chinese, "Mt. Lu" is known as "Lushan." It is often translated as "Mount Lushan" or "Lushan Mountain."

23. The "broad, long tongue" is one of the thirty-two excellent marks of the Buddha. These thirty-two marks of excellence are the remarkable physical characteristics possessed by a Buddha, the symbols of qualities attained at the highest level of cultivation.

24. The "pure body" refers to one's intrinsic nature that is without defilements.

25. The Chinese word *cheng* means "a weighing scale."

26. The name of the temple, "Longhu," means "dragon and tiger."

27. The Chinese term *genji*, translated here as "capacity," means one's "root potential."

28. The Chinese term *genxing*, translated here as "capabilities," refers to one's "root nature."

29. The passing of "autumns and winters" means the passing of "years."

30. Hanyang is a city in Hubei Province on the Yangzi River.

31. "Yingwu" means "parrot," and "Huanghe" means "yellow crane."

32. The Chinese term *shigu* refers to an unmarried female member of the sangha who has not renounced.

33. The Tang Dynasty lasted from 618-907 C.E., and is considered one of the greatest eras of Chinese civilization in both religion and the arts. The Tang Dynasty was the golden age of Chinese Buddhism, during which Buddhism flourished and became the national religion. Many achievements occurred during this era, most notably the translation of sutras.

34. The number 108 is significant in Buddhism, and refers to the 108 defilements.

35. Buddhism denies the existence of a permanent soul or an unchanging entity that transmigrates from one life to another. What transmigrates is the existence that is subject to the Law of Cause and Effect and the Law of Karma.

36. "Habitual tendencies" are the patterns developed by actions throughout lifetimes, and are passed on from one life to the next.

37. The *conglin*, translated here as "Chinese monastic community," literally means "forest of trees." It can also mean a "community of Buddhist practitioners" or a monastery.

38. According to traditional accounts, Baizhang established an early set of rules for Chan monastic discipline called, "The Monastic Regulations of Baizhang" or the "Pure Rules of Huaihai."

39. The phrase "life has the ignorance" means that once someone is reborn, he is ignorant of his previous life.

40. The Liang Dynasty lasted from 502-557 C.E. The only famous ruler of this period is Emperor Wu of Liang who was known for his Buddhist faith and poetry rather than for political success.

41. The Qing Dynasty lasted from 1644-1912 C.E. This dynasty was the outcome of a successful invasion by the Manchus, the second foreign ethnic group to rule the whole of China. During this dynasty, the emperors believed in Lamaism (Tibetan Buddhism).

42. The "purple *kasaya*" is the robe of an Imperial Master, presented to an accomplished monk by the emperor.

43. The phrase "in the West" refers to "India" because Buddhism was carried from west to east, from India to China.

44. The line "message coming from the West" alludes to the transmission of the Dharma from the West to the East.

45. The guest master in a monastery is in charge of receiving and attending to guests.

46. In Japanese, this temple is known as "Daitoku-ji Temple." The word *ji* means "temple."

47. The phrase "body and mind dropped off" describes the experience of letting go of attachments to body and mind.

48. In Chinese, "Mt. Gui" is known as "Guishan." It is sometimes translated as "Guishan Mountain" or "Mount Guishan."

49. Confucianism is a Chinese ethical and philosophical system that developed from the teachings of the Chinese sage Confucius. It is a philosophy of moral, social, religious, and political thought that has had tremendous influence on the history of Chinese civilization.

50. The Song Dynasty lasted from 920-1278 C.E., and is divided into two periods: the Northern Song and the Southern Song. During this time, Buddhism experienced a period of consolidation of the schools. In addition, some features of Confucianism and Daoism were integrated with Buddhism, giving Chinese Buddhism its unique characteristics.

51. The term "Dharma transmission" refers to the act of passing the Chan lineage from master to disciple.

52. The "sweet dew" refers to the Dharma.

53. Bodhidharma was not encouraging Shenguang to cut off his arm. Shenguang cut off his arm to demonstrate his sincerity and resolve to Bodhidharma.

54. During the Tang Dynasty, the government limited the number of people becoming monastics by instituting examinations. One such exam required a candidate to memorize and demonstrate an understanding of a number of Buddhist scriptures.

55. The phrase "propagate the bodhi seeds of the Buddha" alludes to spreading the Buddha's teachings, the seeds of enlightenment.

56. The Chinese term *duanzuo*, translated here as "sitting upright," means to "sit properly" or "sit mindfully."

57. The "light" refers to one of the thirty-two excellent marks of the Buddha. It is a curl of hair between the eyebrows that emits a beam of light to illuminate the world.

58. The "eight winds" are eight kinds of states that we encounter in our lives-praise, ridicule, slander, fame, self-interest, decline, suffering, and joy. They are able to influence our emotions, and therefore, are described as winds.

59. A play on words. In Chinese, *fangpi*, translated here as "fart," also means "nonsense."

60. The "man outside the gate" refers to one who has not seen the Way.

61. The "family treasure" is our Buddha nature. What Yantou means is that what comes from outside is not our original nature.

62. The term "phenomena" describes the conditioned dharmas in the world that are impermanent and subject to change. The term "principle" refers to the general truths or principles that govern phenomenal reality. Since "principle" interacts with "phenomena" without mutual obstruction, they are able to enter into and penetrate one another without losing their essence. Therefore, all phenomena manifest one principle, and this one principle underlies everything in the world of phenomena.

63. This passage is from the *Confucian Analects*, bk. VII, chap. XVIII.

64. The summer retreat is a practice that has been passed down as the "rainy season retreat" since Sakyamuni Bud-

dha's time in India. It refers to the period when Buddhist monks stopped their travels and outdoor activities for the duration of the summer rainy season and gathered at a sheltered location to devote themselves to study and discipline.

65. The Later Han of the Five Dynasties Period lasted from 947-950 C.E. and was the fourth of the Five Dynasties. The Later Han was a tumultuous period marked by continuous wars and division in the country.

66. "Truth" means the supramundane truth

67. According to Chan tradition, Bodhidharma's robe and bowl were passed down from patriarch to patriarch until their transmission from Fifth Patriarch Hongren to Sixth Patriarch Huineng.

68. This line alludes to meeting during the time Maitreya Buddha descends to our world to discourse on the Dharma and liberate sentient beings.

69. The Chinese word *xiao*, translated here as "take," can also mean to "to exhaust." Pei Wende is commenting on whether the monks had enough merit to exhaust his efforts.

70. The Chinese word *xiao* is the same word used in the previous verse. Translated here as "take on," it is used to mean "to bear" or "to hold."

71. This passage is from *The Works of Mencius*, pt. II, bk. VI, chap. XV.

72. The term "lower realms" refers to the realms of animals, hungry ghosts, and hell beings.

73. The term "higher realms" refers to the realms of humans, *asuras*, and heavenly beings.

74. The *sravakas* and *pratyeka-buddhas* still have attachments to good Dharma.

75. In Baizhang's metaphor, he is comparing Guishan to an insect eating wood that unintentionally creates a Chinese character as it eats. Baizhang means that Guishan occasionally hits the mark with his answers.

76. In Chinese, *fuchuan* means a "capsized boat."

77. In Japanese, "Eihei Temple" is known as "Eihei-ji Temple." The word *ji* means "temple." The Eihei Temple is the great head temple of the Soto Sect in Fukui Prefecture, founded in 1243 by Dogen-zenji, the founder of the Soto Sect. It is one of the two great head temples of the Soto Sect.

78. A catty is a unit of measurement in China that is equal to about one-and-a-half pounds (680 grams).

79. The Great Peng is a mythological bird of fantastic size that is comparable to the roc.

80. The phrase "make connections with others" is also translated as "make affinity with others."

81. The name "Xuanji" literally means "weaving loom."

82. The name "Xuefeng" literally means "snowy peak."

83. "Not even a thread" also means to be completely free from worries or cares; without attachments.

84. The *gongan* appears in the *Wumen Guan*, case 2.

85. The Chinese word *mei*, translated here as "ignorant" also means "obscure" or "go against." Baizhang's turning word, "They're not ignorant of cause and effect," means that when one understands cause and effect, one will not go against it.

86. "Two banners in competition" is sometimes translated as "Two faces of a single die."

87. The head gardener in a monastery is the one responsible for the monastics who do the gardening.

88. The *gongan* of "Zhaozhou's tea" appears in the *Xu Zang Jing*, vol. 65, no. 1295, fasc. 20, p. 594. The *gongan* of "Yunmen's cakes" appears in the *Blue Cliff Record*, case 77.

89. The terms "heaven and earth" are *qian kun* in Chinese.

90. The "four imperial persecutions" refers to the complete suppression of Buddhism carried out on four occasions from the fifth through the tenth century by four Chinese emperors. They are: 1) the persecution by Emperor Taiwu of the Northern Wei Dynasty, a believer in Daoism; 2) the persecution by Emperor Wu of the Northern Zhou Dynasty, enacted twice, in 574 and 577; Wu also abolished Daoism, prompting Buddhists to define this time as marking the beginning of the Latter Day of the Law in China; 3) the persecution in 845 by Emperor Wuzong of the Tang Dynasty, which was instigated by Daoists; and 4) the persecution in 955 by Emperor Shizong of the Later Zhou Dynasty, in which thousands of temples were destroyed.

91. The emperor is Emperor Huizong of the Song Dynasty.

92. The Ming Dynasty lasted from 1368-1644 C.E. Compared with other Chinese dynasties, Buddhism declined during the Ming, but there were still some great masters like Master Lianchi to inherit the Dharma transmission.

93. "When you extinguish the fire of the mind, it is cool" means that once you extinguish the fire of the mind, you have entered *samadhi*.

94. The *gongan* of "Zhaozhou's *Wu*" refers to "Do dogs have Buddha nature or not?" It can be found in the *Wumen Guan*, case 1.

Glossary of Buddhist Terms

Amitabha Buddha: Literally "He of Immeasurable Light." In Mahayana Buddhism, Amitabha is considered one of the most important Buddhas and is known as The Buddha of the Western Pure Land. He is sometimes referred to as Amita Buddha or Amitayus Buddha (the Buddha of Infinite Light). It is said that he possesses infinite merits resulting from good deeds over countless past lives as a bodhisattva named Dharmakara, and he vowed to purify a realm for those who desire to seek rebirth there by earnestly reciting his name. In China, he is known as *Amituo Fo*.

Avalokitesvara Bodhisattva: Literally "He Who Hears the Sounds of the World." In Mahayana Buddhism, Avalokitesvara is considered one of the great bodhisattvas and is known as the Bodhisattva of Compassion. He can manifest himself in any form necessary to help any being. In China, he is usually portrayed in female form and is known as *Guanyin Pusa*.

awakening: (Chin., *wu*). A distinction should be made between awakening to the Way (great awakening) and attaining the Way (attaining enlightenment). To experience an awakening through Chan is to see one's nature and comprehend the true nature of phenomena. When a practitioner has attained awakening, it does not mean that his afflictions and attachments are completely eliminated. Only after becoming a Buddha can one be said to have truly attained the Way.

bhiksu: The male members of the Buddhist *sangha* who have renounced household life and received full ordination.

bhiksuni: The female members of the Buddhist *sangha* who have renounced household life and received full ordination.

bodhi: Literally "awakened" or "enlightened." In the state of enlightenment, one is awakened to the true nature of self; one is enlightened to one's own Buddha nature.

bodhi seat: The name given to the seat or place under the Bodhi tree where Sakyamuni Buddha attained enlightenment. It is also known as "the diamond throne" (Skt., *vajrasana*).

bodhisattva: Literally an "enlightening being" or a "sentient being who is seeking enlightenment." A bodhisattva is a being who is seeking the attainment of Buddhahood or liberation, and one who practices all *paramitas*. Bodhisattvas vow to remain in the world to help others achieve enlightenment. The bodhisattva ideal is the defining feature of Mahayana Buddhism.

bodhisattva vow: In Mahayana Buddhism, practitioners vow to seek the bodhi mind and liberate all sentient beings by cultivating the six *paramitas*.

Brahman: A member of the highest of the four castes of Vedic society. They were traditionally the teachers and interpreters of religious knowledge, and the priests who acted as intermediaries between gods, the world, and humans. In ancient Indian society, they were the only group allowed to change and perform the rituals of worship.

Buddha: Literally "The Awakened One." As a generic term, it is used to refer to one who has achieved enlightenment and attained complete liberation from the cycle of existence. It is more commonly used to refer to Sakyamuni Buddha, the historical founder of Buddhism.

Buddha nature: (Skt., *buddhata*). The inherent nature that exists in all beings. Since all beings possess Buddha nature, they all have the capability to achieve Buddhahood.

Buddha Way: The path leading to supreme enlightenment and Buddhahood. See *the Way*.

Buddhakaya: Literally the "body" of the Buddha. It is the corporeal manifestation of the historical Buddha.

cause and effect: (Skt., *hetu-phala*). This is the most basic doctrine of Buddhism, which explains the formation of all relations and connections in the world. This law means that the arising of each and every phenomenon is due to its own causes and conditions, and the actual form, or appearance, of all phenomena is in effect.

Chan: The Chinese transliteration of the Sanskrit term, *dhyana*; it refers to meditative concentration.

Chan School: A school of Chinese Buddhism founded by Bodhidharma in China. It emphasizes the cultivation of intrinsic wisdom, and teaches that enlightenment is clarifying the mind and seeing one's own true nature. A major tenet of the Chan School is that the Dharma is wordlessly transmitted from mind to mind.

chiliocosm: In Buddhist cosmology, Mt. Sumeru and its four great continents, nine mountains, and eight oceans form one small world. One thousand of these worlds form a small *chiliocosm*.

conditioned dharma: (Skt., *samskrta*). It describes all the various phenomena in the world that are impermanent and subject to change.

cycle of birth and death: (Skt., *samsara* or *jatimarana*). It is also known as transmigration. When sentient beings die, they are reborn into one of the six realms of existence (the realms of heaven, human, *asura*, animals, hungry ghost, and hell). The cycle is continuous and endless due to the karmic result of one's deeds.

delusion: It is the same as ignorance, a lack of awareness of the true nature or Buddha nature of things. According to the Buddhist perspective, we are deluded by our attachments to phenomena and our senses.

dependent origination: (Skt., *pratitya-samutpada*). The central principle that phenomena do not come into existence independently but only as a result of causes and conditions; therefore, no phenomena possesses an independent self-nature. This concept is also referred to as interdependence. The twelve factors of dependent origination are: ignorance, mental formation, consciousness, mind and body, the six senses, contact, feeling, craving, grasping, becoming, birth, and aging and death.

Dharma: Literally "law." It usually refers to the teachings of the Buddha. When capitalized, it means: 1) the ultimate truth and 2) the teachings of the Buddha. When it appears in lowercase, dharma refers to anything that can be thought of, experienced, or named; close in meaning to "phenomena."

Dharma brother: A fellow disciple of the same master.

Dharma nature: The original essence of all phenomena. It is used interchangeably with "suchness" and "reality."

Dharmakaya: It is also known as Dharma-body; refers to the true nature of a Buddha and also to the absolute Dharma that the Buddha attained. It is one of three bodies possessed by a Buddha.

dharma realm: (Skt., *dharma-dhatu*). It refers to a particular plane of existence in which all phenomena arise, abide, and extinguish.

Diamond Sutra: (Skt., *Vajracchedika-prajna-paramita-sutra*; Chin. *Jinggang Jing*). The sutra sets forth the doctrine of emptiness and the perfection of wisdom. The *Diamond Sutra* is named thus because the perfection of wisdom cuts through delusion like a diamond.

emptiness: (Skt., *sunyata*). A basic concept in Buddhism that means everything existing in the world is due to dependent origination and has no permanent self or substance.

five aggregates: (Skt., *skandas*). They make up the totality of sentient existence: form, feeling, perception, mental formation, and consciousness.

five desires: The desires that arise from the objects of the five senses: form, sound, smell, taste, and touch. Also known as the five sensual pleasures, they can refer to the desires for wealth, sexual love, food and drink, fame, and sleep.

Five Precepts: (Skt., *pancasila*). The fundamental principles of conduct and discipline that were established by the Buddha for wholesome and harmonious living. They are: 1) do not kill; 2) do not steal; 3) do not lie; 4) do not engage in sexual misconduct; and 5) do not take intoxicants.

Flower Ornament Sutra: (Skt., *Avatamsaka-sutra*; Chin., *Huayan Jing*). The complete Sanskrit title is *Buddhavatam-saka-mahavaipulya-sutra*. It is traditionally believed that this sutra was taught to bodhisattvas and other high spiritual beings while the Buddha was in *samadhi*. The major teachings in the Huayan School are based on this sutra.

four great elements: (Skt., *catvari-mahabhutani*). In Buddhism, all matters in the world are composed of the elements of earth, water, fire, and wind.

Four Noble Truths: (Skt., *catvari-arya-satyani*). A fundamental Buddhist teaching about the nature and existence of suffering: 1) the truth of suffering; 2) the truth of the cause of suffering; 3) the truth of the cessation of suffering; and 4) the path leading to the cessation of suffering.

Four Reliances: (Skt., *catvari-pratisharana*). They are four guidelines to keep Buddhists on the right path: 1) rely on the Dharma, not on people; 2) rely on wisdom, not on knowledge; 3) rely on meaning, not on words; and 4) rely on definitive meaning, not on provisional meaning.

gatha: Verse; a means of exposition in the Buddhist scriptures.

General Skanda: He is regarded as one of the eight divine protectors in Chinese Buddhism, a devoted guardian of Buddhist monasteries who protects the Dharma and the objects of the Dharma. Known in Chinese as *Weituo*, he is usually depicted as a majestic general fully clad in armor.

gongan: Literally "public notice" in Chinese, it originally referred to a legal precedent. However, this term was adopted by the Chan tradition to refer to a phrase, or a question and answer exchange, which points to an essential paradox. The contemplation of a *gongan* is aimed at transcending logical or conceptual assumptions in order to intuit the nature of emptiness. This term is known in Japanese as *koan*.

Great Vehicle: See *Mahayana*.

Heart Sutra: (Skt., *Mahaprajnaparamita-hridaya-sutra*; Chin., *Xin Jing*). It is one of the most important sutras of Mahayana Buddhism and particularly in China and Japan. The *Heart Sutra* emphasizes in a particularly clear and concise way the teaching of emptiness.

Hinayana: Literally "Small Vehicle." From the Mahayana perspective, the Hinayana is called the "Small Vehicle" because, in contrast to the Mahayana, it has self-liberation as a goal rather than the liberation of all sentient beings.

huatou: Literally "word head." It is the point or key line of a *gongan*, the word or phrase in which the *gongan* resolves itself when one struggles with it as a means of Chan training. A *gongan* can have only one, or several *huatou*, and the *huatou* can consist of a single word or be a long expression.

Imperial Master: (Chin., *guoshi*). The teacher of a nation; honorific title for the Buddhist teacher of a Chinese emperor.

intrinsic nature: (Skt., *svabhava*). One's own original nature; Buddha nature.

kalpa: A measuring unit of time in ancient India; a *kalpa* is an immense and inconceivable length of time. Buddhism has adapted this term to refer to the period of time between the creation and re-creation of the worlds.

karma: Literally "action" or "deed." The term is used to denote the Law of Cause and Effect. All deeds, whether good or bad, produce effects. The effects may be experienced instantly, or they may not come into fruition for many years or even many lifetimes.

kasaya: A monastic's robe or cassock.

liberation: (Skt., *vimoksa*). It is a state free from all afflictions, suffering, and the cycle of birth and death.

Lotus Sutra: (Skt., *Saddharmapundarika-sutra*; Chin., *Miaofa Lianhua Jing*). One of the most important sutras of Mahayana Buddhism, and is especially popular in China and Japan. The *Lotus Sutra* contains the essential teachings of the Mahayana: the doctrines of the transcendental nature of the Buddha and of the possibility of universal liberation. It is said to have been expounded by Sakyamuni Buddha at the end of his period of teaching. The schools of Tiantai are based on this teaching.

Mahayana: Literally "Great Vehicle." It is one of the two main traditions of Buddhism, which stresses that helping other sentient beings attain enlightenment is more important than self-liberation. The vow to strive for the benefit of all sentient beings is embodied in the Mahayana ideal of the compassionate bodhisattva.

Maitreya Bodhisattva: Literally "The One of Loving-kindness." The future Buddha. It is said that after Sakyamuni Buddha's teachings disappear from this world, Maitreya, moved by compassion, will manifest in our world as a spiritual teacher. He currently presides over Tusita Heaven, where he is expounding the Dharma to heavenly beings in the inner palace. In China, he is known as *Mile Pusa*.

Manjusri Bodhisattva: Literally "He of Wondrous Merit and Virtue." In Mahayana Buddhism, he is regarded as the Bodhisattva of Wisdom, and is closely associated with knowledge and learning. A male bodhisattva, he is depicted wielding a flaming sword in his right hand, which cuts through ignorance and wrong views. In China, he is known as *Wenshu Pusa*.

Mara: The term is used to refer to the devil or demons.

merit: (Skt., *punya*). The accumulation of beneficial consequences, good karma.

Middle Way: (Skt., *madhyama-pratipad*). The path taught by Sakyamuni Buddha, which transcends all extremes and leads to liberation.

mind: (Chin., *xin*). The Chinese character *xin* can be translated as "heart" or "mind." In Chan, it means the mind of a person in the sense of all his powers of consciousness, mind, heart, and spirit. It is the mind beyond the distinction between mind and matter, intrinsic nature, or true nature.

mind-ground: (Chin., *xindi*). It is another term for "mind," from which all things spring. The mind is compared to the ground, which has two characteristics: it sustains everything and it does not discriminate.

mind's eye: (Skt., *urna*). A symbol of enlightenment, it is one of the thirty-two marks of a Buddha. Also known as the Eye of Wisdom, it is a curl of hair between the eyebrows that emits a beam of light to illuminate the world.

Mt. Sumeru: According to Buddhist cosmology, it is a sacred mountain that is the center of the world.

Mt. Wutai: Literally "Five Terrace Mountain." It is one of the four most famous mountains in China and a very important pilgrimage site for Chinese Buddhists who venerate Manjusri Bodhisattva.

mundane truth: (Skt., *samvrti-satya*). Worldly truth that is based on the common understanding of ordinary people and is subject to the Law of Cause and Effect.

nirvana: Literally "extinguishing" or "extinction." In Buddhism, it refers to the absolute extinction of individual existence or of all afflictions and desires; the state of liberation beyond birth and death. It is also the final goal and attainment in Buddhism.

Nirvana Sutra: (Skt., *Mahaparinirvana-sutra*; Chin., *Niepan Jing*). A collection of Mahayana sutras recording the teachings that Sakyamuni Buddha expounded immediately before his death or describing the events surrounding his entry into nirvana. An important influence on the Chan tradition, it deals primarily with the doctrine of Buddha nature and presents itself as providing the correct understanding for teachings such as no-self and emptiness.

no-self: (Skt., *anatman*). A fundamental concept in Buddhism that means all phenomena and beings in the world have no real, permanent, and substantial self. Everything arises, abides, changes, and extinguishes based on the Law of Dependent Origination.

non-duality: (Skt., *advaya*). One of Sakyamuni Buddha's teachings, it espouses the doctrines of no extremes, no distinctions, and equality.

novice monk: (Skt., *sramanera*). A monk who has not yet received full ordination but has undertaken to observe the ten precepts.

ordinary mind: (Chin., *pingchang xin*). The ordinary mind is the mind that is unmoved by disturbances. It does not function with intentional action but is free from any attachment or differentiation. It is often translated as the "equanimous mind" and "everyday mind."

original face: (Chin., *benlai mianmu*). The true self or Buddha nature.

phenomena: See *conditioned dharma*.

prajna: Literally "wisdom." As the highest form of wisdom, *prajna* is the wisdom of insight into emptiness, which is the true nature of all phenomena. The realization of *prajna* also implies the attainment of enlightenment, and is in this sense one of the six *paramitas* or perfections of the bodhisattva path. It is sometimes referred to by the compound term *prajna-wisdom*.

prajna-wisdom: The highest form of wisdom. See *prajna*.

Prajna Sutras: (Skt., *Prajnaparamita-sutras*; Chin., *Poruo Jing*). The term refers to the *Sutras of Wisdom* in the *Tripitaka*. The shorter versions of these sutras include the *Heart Sutra* and the *Diamond Sutra*. The longest version of the sutras is the *Sutra on the Perfection of Great Wisdom*.

pratyeka-buddha: Literally "solitary awakened one." It refers to those who awaken to the Truth through their own efforts in an age without the presence of a Buddha. The *pratyeka-buddha* seeks enlightenment through the contemplation of the Law of Dependent Origination for his or her own liberation.

precepts: The rules of moral conduct for all Buddhists. There are separate precepts for monastics and lay practitioners. However, in the Mahayana tradition there is a special category referred to as the "Bodhisattva Precepts" followed by practitioners.

pure land: It is another term for a Buddha realm, which is established by the vows and cultivation of one who has achieved enlightenment.

Pure Land School: A school of Chinese Buddhism founded by Huiyuan on Mt. Lu in the year 402. It is a devotional form of Buddhism that is centered on Amitabha Buddha. Pure Land Buddhism teaches that through faith in Amitabha, one can enter the Western Pure Land of Ultimate Bless from which liberation will be easier to attain.

relics: (Skt., *sarira*). The remains of the historical Buddha, as well as those of other Buddhas, bodhisattvas, and even some disciples of the Buddha. They often appear as small bead-like remains found in the ashes after cremation, and are objects of veneration in certain areas of the world.

renunciation: (Skt., *nekkhamma*). One of the most fundamental concepts in Buddhism, it refers to a process of reducing the attachments that our emotion of desire creates. Outward renunciation is when a man or woman leaves the household life to become a monk or a nun. True renunciation is a matter of the mind rather than the body, and is a renunciation of the world of desires within. Ultimate renunciation is the renunciation of the "self" in its entirety.

samadhi: Literally "establish" or "make firm." The highest state of mind achieved through meditation, chanting, reciting the Buddha's name, and other practices, in which the mind has reached ultimate concentration and is not subject to thoughts and distractions, thereby entering a state of inner serenity.

Samantabhadra Bodhisattva: Literally "He Who Is Universally Virtuous." In Mahayana Buddhism, he is venerated as the protector of all who teach the Dharma. According to the *Avatamsaka Sutra,* he made the ten great vows which are the basis of a bodhisattva. In China, he is sometimes depicted with feminine characteristics riding on an elephant with six tusks and is known as *Puxian Pusa.*

sangha: The Buddhist community. In a broad sense, it includes both monastics and laypeople. In a stricter sense, it refers to the monastic community or to those of advanced spiritual attainment.

Sakyamuni Buddha: (581-501 B.C.E.) Literally "Sage of the Sakyas." The historical founder of Buddhism. He was born the prince of Kapilavastu, son of King Suddhodana. At the age of twenty-nine, he left the royal palace and his family to search for the meaning of existence. At the age of thirty-five, he attained enlightenment under the Bodhi tree. He then spent the next forty-five years expounding his teachings, which include the Four Noble Truths, the Noble Eightfold Path, the Law of Cause and Effect, and dependent origination. At the age of eighty, he entered the state of *parinirvana.*

seal of approval: (Chin., *yinzheng*). A formal acknowledgment or legitimate seal of confirmation of a student's completion of Chan training. It does not imply mastery, merely a sign by the master of being satisfied with the student's level of understanding.

sentient beings: (Skt., *sattvas*). All beings with consciousness, including celestial beings, *asuras,* humans, animals, hungry ghosts, and hell beings. From the Mahayana perspective, all sentient beings inherently have Buddha nature and therefore possess the capacity to attain enlightenment.

Seven Ancient Buddhas: (Skt., *sapta-buddha*). The term refers to Sakyamuni Buddha and the six Buddhas who preceded his arrival: 1) Vipasyin; 2) Sikhin; 3) Visvabhu; 4) Krakucchanda; 5) Kanakamuni; 6) Kasyapa; and 7) Sakyamuni. They are also collectively known as the Seven Buddhas of the Past.

seven locations: (Chin., *qichu*). In the *Surangama Sutra,* Ananda and Sakyamuni Buddha have a dialogue about the location of the mind; that is, discriminating consciousness. Ananda puts forth seven hypothetical locations, which the Buddha refutes in turn: 1) the mind resides in the body; 2) the mind resides outside the body; 3) the mind is hidden in the sensory faculty; 4) the mind is located inside the body when we close our eyes; 5) the mind is located where causes and conditions come together and where existence arises; 6) the mind is located between the sensory faculties and the six dusts; and 7) the mind is non-abiding. The Buddha concludes by telling Ananda that the mind cannot be located in any specific place.

signal hand bell: (Chin., *yinqing*). A Dharma instrument. The small bell, which is both held and tapped with a mallet by the same hand, is used while chanting. It has also been translated as "inverted bell."

six consciousnesses: (Skt., *sadvijnana*). The six kinds of perception that occur when the six sense organs make contact with their respective objects: 1) eye-consciousness; 2) ear-consciousness; 3) nose-consciousness; 4) tongue-consciousness; 5) body-consciousness; and 6) mind-consciousness.

six dusts: (Skt., *sad visayah*). The six objects reflected by the six sense organs, which then produce the six consciousnesses: 1) sight; 2) sound; 3) smell; 4) taste; 5) touch; and 6) phenomena.

six sense organs: (Skt., *sad indriyani*). The eyes, ears, nose, tongue, body, and mind.

skillful means: (Skt., *upaya-kausalya*). It is the notion that the Buddha teaches skillfully and applies different practices and teachings because all beings have various different capacities, and must be led to the path toward awakening through appropriate approaches. In Mahayana Buddhism, skillful means is a method employed by Buddhas and bodhisattvas to benefit sentient beings.

Small Vehicle: It means the vehicle that can only carry a few people. This term is used to refer to one who only focuses on self-cultivation. See *Hinayana*.

sravaka: Literally "hearer." It refers to one who has attained *arhatship* after hearing the Buddha's teachings. Upon fulfilling the *arhat* ideal, the *sravaka* chooses not to remain in the cycle of rebirth to benefit all sentient beings and instead enters nirvana.

suchness: (Skt., *tathata* or *bhutatathata*). A term for the true nature of all things; the pure, original essence of all phenomena.

supernatural powers: It refers to that which is beyond or above the natural, and cannot be controlled by natural law. In Buddhism, there are six kinds of supernatural powers: 1) psychic traveling; 2) clairaudience (deva-ear); 3) clairvoyance (deva-eye); 4) mental telepathy; 5) knowledge of past and future; 6) and extinction of outflows.

supramundane truth: (Skt., *paramartha-satya*). The supreme and absolute truth, which is transcends arising, abiding, decaying, and extinguishing.

Surangama Sutra: (Skt., *Suramgama-samadhi-sutra*; Chin., *Lengyan Jing*). It exercised a great influence on the development of Mahayana Buddhism in China. The *Surangama Sutra* emphasizes the power of *samadhi* through which enlightenment can be attained and the importance of the precepts as a foundation for the Way.

sutra: Literally "threaded together." It refers to the collections of the discourses taught by the Buddha, and recorded by his disciples for all to follow in their practice. The direct attribution of the teachings to the Buddha is implied in the opening line of each sutra, "Thus have I heard."

Tathagata: (Chin., *rulai*). Literally "The One Thus-Come," it is one of the ten epithets of Buddha. *Tathagata* means the one who has attained full realization of suchness; the one with the absolute, so that he neither comes from anywhere nor goes anywhere. According to Buddhist tradition, it was the title Sakyamuni Buddha used when referring to himself.

Tathagatagarbha: Literally "the womb of the Tathagata." It refers to the Dharmakaya of the Tathagata that is hidden within all beings. The term is synonymous with "intrinsic nature" or "original nature."

ten directions: (Skt., *dasa disah*). This term is used to refer to everywhere, indicating the eight points of the compass (north, west, east, south, southeast, southwest, northeast, and northwest) plus the zenith and nadir

Tendai: (Chin., *tiantai*). Japanese form of the Chinese Tiantai School. It was brought to Japan from China by the Japanese monk Saicho in 805. There are no essential doctrinal differences between the Chinese and Japanese forms of the school.

Three Dharma Seals: Sakyamuni Buddha taught that everything in the world is marked by three characteristics: 1) all phenomena are impermanent; 2) all phenomena do not have a substantial self; and 3) nirvana is perfect tranquility. They are also known as the Three Marks of Existence.

three realms: (Skt., *trayo dhatavah*). The realms where sentient beings reside and transmigrate: 1) the realm of sense-desires; 2) the realm of form; and 3) the realm of formlessness.

trichiliocosm: (Skt., *tri-sahasra-maha-sahasra-loka-dhatu*). It refers to the thousand-cubed great-thousand-world.

three time periods: Also known as the three periods of time, this term is used to refer to the past, present, and future.

Tiantai: Literally "School of the Celestial Platform." A school of Chinese Buddhism founded by Master Zhiyi on Mt. Tiantai during the Sui Dynasty (589-618). Zhiyi adopted a system of comparative classification, which organized all the Buddhist sutras into Five Periods and Eight Teachings. The Tiantai School bases its tenets on the *Lotus Sutra* and develops Nagarjuna's teaching of the three levels of truth.

tonsure: The act of shaving the head or part of the head, especially as a preliminary to becoming a member of a monastic order.

transferring merits: (Skt., *parinamanam*). The act of transferring to others the merits one gains through Buddhist practice. Transferring merits to the departed is based on the belief that upon a person's death, his karma will determine where he is reborn. Friends and relatives can transfer merits gained from doing meritorious deeds to the departed, and thereby release those reborn in the lower realms from their suffering.

Triple Gem: (Skt., *tri-ratna*). This term refers to Buddha, the Dharma, and the Sangha; it is also called the Triple Jewel or the Three Jewels. The Buddha is the fully awakened or enlightened one, the Dharma is the teachings imparted by the Buddha, and the Sangha is the community of monastics.

turning word: (Chin., *zhuanyu*). A word, when spoken and heard just at the right time and place, that has the power to serve as a turning point in one's life.

unconditioned dharma: (Skt., *asamskrta*). It describes that which is not subject to the Law of Cause and Effect, nor the Law of Dependent Origination.

wandering monk: (Chin., *yunshui seng*). Literally "clouds and water monk." It refers to a wandering Buddhist monk who travels unbounded like the "clouds and water" in search of teachers and the Way.

the Way: (Chin., *dao*). The path leading to liberation taught by the Buddha.

without outflow: (Skt., *anasrava*; Chin., *wulou*). The Chinese word *lou* means "leak" or "leaking." In Buddhism, "leaks" or "outflows" represent afflictions. The state of "without outflows" refers to the state of liberation. The term "without outflows" can also refer to those dharmas free from afflictions and leading to liberation.

wooden fish: (Chin., *muyu*). A Dharma instrument. The wooden percussion instrument is used by monastics of the Mahayana Buddhist tradition. It serves as a signal to start and end a meditation session and it is used to keep rhythm in chanting. The "fish" is symbolic of wakefulness and awareness in Buddhist practice; since fish do not have eyelids, their eyes remain open even when they sleep.

Yama: The ruler of the hell realms who rewards beings with the painful results of their karmic choices. However, Yama does not function as the judge who decides the type, duration, nature, or place of punishment. That determination is made by the Law of Karma.

Zen: (Jap., *zenna* or *zenno*, from the *Chin., channa* or *chan*, a Chin. version of Skt. *dhyana*). See *Chan*. The Zen School is the Japanese form of the Chinese Chan School. As Chan gradually waned in China, the different lineages flowed into Korea and Japan. The Linji (Jap., *Rinzai*) lineage reached Japan in the twelfth century and the Caodong (Jap., *Soto*) lineage at the beginning of the thirteenth century. Japanese masters of these two traditions, together with a few Chinese Chan masters who were invited to Japan, founded the Zen tradition.

Biographies of the Chan Masters

This list includes the names of Chan masters who appear in these one hundred stories. The names appear first as they do in the story, followed by their full name in parentheses. The names of Chan masters traditionally consisted of two parts: the geographic name and Dharma name. In ancient China, Chan masters commonly took the name of the mountain, monastery, or town where they lived and taught; their teachers gave them their Dharma names. In the case of Japanese masters, the Chinese transliteration of their names is shown in parentheses.

Baizhang Huaihai (*Baizhang Huaihai*; 720-814). Dharma successor of Mazu Daoyi. He resided and taught on Mt. Baizhang, established the monastic regulations for Chan monasteries, and practiced the agricultural Chan lifestyle. Huangbo Xiyun and Guishan Lingyou were among his disciples. He was given the posthumous name "Chan Master Dazhi" (Great Wisdom).

Bankei (*Bankei Eitaku*; Chin., *Pangui*; 1622-1693). Dharma successor of Bokuo Sogyu in the Rinzai lineage of Japanese Zen Buddhism. He became a monk at sixteen under Umpo Zenjo of Zuio Temple, founded Ryumon Temple, and was appointed abbot of Myoshin Temple by imperial decree. He was posthumously given the rare imperial title of "Kokushi" (Imperial Master).

Bodhidharma (*Bodhidharma*; Chin., *Puti Damo*; d. 535). First Patriarch of Chinese Chan Buddhism. Dharma successor of Prajnatara, the Twenty-eighth Patriarch of Indian Buddhism. According to traditional Chan accounts, he traveled from Southern India to China, settled at Shaolin Temple on Mt. Song, and spent nine years in meditation facing the wall of a cave. Shenguang Huike, Daoyu, Daofu, and Bhiksuni Zongchi were among his disciples. He was given the posthumous name "Great Master Yuanjue" (Perfectly Enlightened).

Chenghao (*Yuquan Chenghao*; 1011-1091). Dharma successor of Beita Siguang. He resided near Mt. Yin in Xiangyang Valley and later moved to Yuquan Temple in Jingzhou.

Ciming (*Ciming Chuyuan* or *Shishuang Chuyuan*; 986-1039). Dharma successor of Fenyang Shanzhao. He resided and taught at several different temples, including Chongsheng Temple on Mt. Shishuang. Yangqi Fanghui and Huanglong Huinan, founders of the two main branches of Linji Chan, were among his many Dharma successors. He was given the posthumous name "Chan Master Ciming" (Compassionate Clarity).

Dadian (*Dadian Baotong*; 732-824). Dharma successor of Shitou Xiqian in the Caoxi lineage of Chinese Chan Buddhism. He was the founder of the Lingshan Chan Monastery. Sanping Yizhong was his Dharma successor.

Dahui Zonggao (*Dahui Zonggao*; 1089-1163). Dharma successor of Yuanwu Keqin in the Yangqi branch of the Linji lineage of Chinese Chan Buddhism. He resided on Mt. Jing, compiled the records of ancient masters in a six-volume collection, and strongly advocated *huatou* practice. Also known as "Master Fori" (Buddha Sun), he was given the posthumous name "Chan Master Pujue" (Universal Awakening).

Danxia (*Danxia Tianran*; 739-824). Dharma successor of Shitou Xiqian. He was a wandering monk who spent much of his life visiting temples and well-known masters. Originally a student of Mazu Daoyi, he was sent to study under Shitou Xiqian and later returned to Mazu's monastery. Cuiwei Wuxue, Jizhou Xingkong, and Daxia Yian were among his disciples. He was given the posthumous name "Chan Master Zhitong" (Wisdom Penetration).

Daokai (*Furong Daokai*; 1043-1118). Dharma successor of Touzi Yiqing in the Caodong lineage of Chinese Chan Buddhism. He underwent a period of exile for refusing the imperial title and honored purple robe presented to him by Emperor Huizong, but later resided and taught at a temple the emperor built for him on Mt. Furong. Danxia Zichun and Chanti Weizhao were among his many disciples.

Daoqian (*Mian Daoqian*; n.d.). Dharma successor of Dahui Zonggao in the Linji lineage of Chinese Chan Buddhism. He resided and taught at Kaishan Temple.

Daoshu (*Shouzhou Daoshu*; n.d.). Disciple of Yuquan Shenxiu, the second generation of Daman Hongren's Dharma successors. He resided near Mt. Sanfeng in Shouzhou.

Daowu Yuanzhi (*Daowu Yuanzhi;* 769-835). Dharma successor of Yaoshan Weiyan in the Qingyuan lineage of Chinese Chan Buddhism. He resided and taught on Mt. Daowu. Many *gongans* in the Chan tradition consist of dialogues between him and Yunyan Tancheng. Also known as "Master Zongzhi," he was given the posthumous name "Master Xiuyi" (Cultivating Oneness).

Dazhu Huihai (*Dazhu Huihai;* n.d.). Dharma successor of Mazu Daoyi. He belonged to the Hongzhou lineage of Chinese Chan Buddhism. He resided and taught the Dharma in Yuezhou.

Deshan (*Deshan Xuanjian;* 782-865). Dharma successor of Longtan Chongxin. He resided on Mt. De, was learned in the *Diamond Sutra,* and his Chan style of teaching was known as "Deshan's stick." Yantou Quanhuo, Xuefeng Yicun, Ruilong Huigong, Quanzhou Waguan, and Shuangliu Weichi were among his disciples. He was given the posthumous name "Chan Master Jianxing" (See the Nature).

Dingzhou (*Liangshan Yuanguan;* n.d.). Disciple of Tongan Guanzhi in the Caodong lineage of Chinese Chan Buddhism. He resided on Mt. Liangshan in Dingzhou. Dayang Jingxuan was his chief disciple.

Dongshan Liangjie (*Dongshan Liangjie;* 807-869). Founder of the Caodong lineage of Chinese Chan Buddhism. Dharma successor of Yunyan Tancheng. He resided and taught on Mt. Dong in Jiangxi. Yunju Daoying, Caoshan Benji, Longya Judun, Huayan Xiujing were among his numerous disciples. He was given the posthumous name "Chan Master Wuben" (Awakening Origin).

Doushuai Congyue (*Doushuai Congyue;* 1044-1091). Dharma successor of Zhenjing Kewen and a monk of the Huanglong branch of the Linji lineage of Chinese Chan Buddhism. He resided and taught at Doushuai Monastery. Shushan Liaochang and Doushuai Huizhao were among his disciples. He was given the posthumous name "Chan Master Zhenji" (True Tranquility).

Eihei Dogen (*Eihei Dogen;* Chin., *Daoyuan;* 1200-1253). Founder of the Soto lineage of Japanese Zen Buddhism. Dharma successor of Butsuju Myozen. He studied Zen under Myozen, traveled to China and received Dharma approval from Tiantong Rujing, and returned to Japan where he later founded Eihei Temple. Author of several works, including *Shobogenzo* (*The Treasury of the Eye of the True Dharma*) *and Eihei Shingi* (*Eihei Rules of Purity*). Also known as Dogen Kigen, he was given the posthumous title "Bussho-dento-kokushi" (Imperial Master Who Spread Buddha Nature to the East).

Ekido (*Sengai Ekido;* Chin., *Zhanyai Yitang* or *Zhuyue Yitang;* 1805-1879). Disciple of Fugai Honko in the Soto lineage of Japanese Zen Buddhism. He served as the abbot of Daihonzan Soji Temple. Daikyu Goyu was his chief disciple.

Foguang (*Wuxue Zuyuan;* Jap., *Bukko Nyoman;* 1226-1286). Dharma successor of Wuzhun Shifan in the Yangqi branch of the Linji lineage of Chinese Chan Buddhism. He was a Chinese master who went to Japan at the invitation of the Kamakura shogunate, where he propagated the Dharma and founded Engaku Temple. Mugai Nyodai was his Dharma successor in Japan. He was given the titles "Chan Master Foguang" (Buddha Light; Jap., Bukko) and "Imperial Master Yuanmian Changzhao" (Complete Eternal Illumination; Jap., Emman-josjo-kokushi).

Foku Weize (*Foku Weize;* 751-830). Dharma successor of Nanyang Huizhong in the Niutou lineage of Chinese Chan Buddhism. He resided at Yankai Vihara in Foku on Mt. Tiantai. Yunju Puzhi was his disciple. He was also known as "Yize."

Foyin (*Foyin Liaoyuan;* 1032-1098). Disciple of Yuantong Juna. He originally studied Chan under Kaixian Shanxian at Kaixian Temple on Mt. Lu, and later became a disciple of Yuantong Juna, residing at Chengtian Temple in Jiangzhou.

Fugai Ekun (*Fugai Ekun;* Chin., *Huixun;* 1568 1664). Zen monk, painter, and calligrapher of the Soto lineage of

Japanese Zen Buddhism. Master at painting Bodhidharma. He spent two decades as a wandering monk after completing his Zen training, briefly served as abbot of Seigan Temple, but gave up the position to be a hermit monk and live in seclusion. This practice of living in mountainside caves earned him the nickname "Ana Fugai" (Cave Fugai).

Gessen (*Gessen Zenne;* Chin., *Yuechuan;* 1702-1781). Belonged to the Jodo school of Japanese Buddhism. He was one of the most prominent painter monks of the late Edo period, and lived in seclusion at Tokian in Musashi-Nagata. Sengai Gibon and Inzan Ien were among his disciples.

Guishan Lingyou (*Guishan Lingyou;* 771-853). Founder of the Guiyang lineage of Chinese Chan Buddhism. Dharma successor of Baizhang Huaihai. He resided on Mt. Dagui for forty years. Many *gongans* consist of dialogues between him and Yangshan. Yangshan Huiji, Xiangyan Zhixian, and Jingshan Hongzhen were among his disciples. He was given the posthumous name "Chan Master Dayuan" (Great Perfection).

Hongren (*Daman Hongren;* 601-675). Fifth Patriarch of the Chinese Chan School. Dharma successor of Dayi Daoxin. He resided and taught on Mt. Pingmao, also known as Mt. Dong. His Dharma successors Dajian Huineng, Yuquan Shenxiu, and Zizhou Zhishen were the founders of the Southern, Northern, and Sichuan Schools of Chan Buddhism.

Hongyi (*Yanyin* or *Hongyi;* 1880-1942). Disciple of Liaowu. He was thirty-eight years old when he became a monk at Daci Temple in Hangzhou. A faithful upholder of traditional codes of Buddhist practice, he was known for his mastery of the *Vinaya,* his essays on Buddhist practice, and his calligraphy. Feng Zikai, the famous Chinese artist and writer, was a close friend and disciple.

Huangbo Xiyun (*Huangbo Xiyun;* d. 850). Dharma successor of Baizhang Huaihai. He resided and taught on Mt. Huangbo and Mt. Tiantai. His teachings were recorded by Pei Xiu in the *Chuanxin Fayao* (*Dharma Essence of Mind Transmission*), an important text in the Chan tradition. Linji Yixuan was one of his many disciples. He was given the posthumous name "Chan Master Duanji" (Severing Limits).

Huineng (*Dajian Huineng;* 638-713). Sixth Patriarch of the Chinese Chan School. Dharma successor of Daman Hongren. The five traditional lineages of Chinese Chan Buddhism trace their origin to him. The main source of information about his life is the *Platform Sutra of the Sixth Patriarch,* a record of his teachings. He resided as abbot at Baolin Monastery near Shaozhou and had twenty-six chief disciples. Among them were Heze Shenhui, Nanyue Huairang, and Qingyuan Xingsi. He was also known as "Caoxi."

Ikkyu (*Ikkyu Sojun;* Chin., *Yixiu Zongchun;* 1394-1481). Dharma successor of Kaso Sodon in the Rinzai lineage of Japanese Zen Buddhism. He received the seal of approval from Kaso, traveled extensively as a wandering monk, served briefly as the abbot of Daitoku Temple by imperial decree, and was famous for his unconventional poetry, calligraphy, and paintings. Shoto Bokusai was his disciple. Also known as "Shuken," he called himself "Kyoun" (Crazy Cloud).

Jianyuan Zhongxing (*Jianyuan Zhongxing;* n.d.). Dharma successor of Daowu Yuanzhi.

Jichin (*Jichin;* Chin., *Cizhen;* 1155-1225). Sixty-second Patriarch of Japanese Tendai Buddhism. He resided at Shoren Temple. As abbot of Shoren Temple, he was also in charge of the Hossho and Modo temples. He was acting as the precept master when Shinran became a monk. He is also widely known by the name of "Jien."

Jingyuan (*Cian Jingyuan;* n.d.). Disciple of Yuanwu Keqin, who was also known as Zhaojue Keqin. He became a monk under Lingshan Xigong, studied the Tiantai doctrines for several years, and then attained great awakening under Yuanwu Keqin. He taught at Huoguo Temple on Mt. Nanming and was also known as "Huguo Cian Jingyuan."

Jinshan Tanying (*Jinshan Tanying;* 989-1060). Disciple of Guyin Yuncong in the Linji lineage of Chinese Chan Buddhism. He resided at Longyou Temple on Mt. Jin and was also known as "Daguan Tanying."

Junji (*Songshan Junji;* n.d.) Little information about this Chan master is known.

Lanzan (*Nanyue Lanzan* or *Mingzan;* n.d.). Dharma successor of Songshan Puji. He lived a humble life of reclusion deep in the forests of Mt. Heng in Hunan during the Tang Dynasty. He was given the posthumous name "Chan Master Daming" (Great Clarity).

Linji (*Linji Yixuan;* d. 867). Founder of the Linji lineage of Chinese Chan Buddhism. Dharma successor of Huang-bo Xiyun. He resided and taught at Linji temple in Hebei. His teaching approach of shouting, known as the "Linji Shout" in the Chan School, was directed at bringing about the moment of awakening. The *Linji Lu* (*Record of Linji*) is a compiled record of his sayings, dialogues, and teachings. He was given the posthumous name "Chan Master Huizhao" (Wise Illumination).

Longtan Chongxin (*Longtan Chongxin;* n.d.). Dharma successor of Tianhuang Daowu. He belonged to the lineage of Qingyuan Xingsi, built Longtan Chan Monastery in Lizhou, and transmitted the Dharma to Deshan Xuanjian.

Mazu Daoyi (*Mazu Daoyi;* 709-788). Founder of the Hongzhou lineage of Chinese Chan Buddhism. Dharma successor of Nanyue Huairang. He traveled throughout China as a wandering monk and settled to teach at Kaiyuan Temple in Zhongling. He is regarded as the first Chan master to use the teaching method of the shout, stick, and glare to awaken his students. Baizhang Huaihai, Damei Fachang, and Nanquan Puyuan were among his many Dharma successors. He was given the posthumous name "Daji" (Great Tranquility).

Mokusen (*Mokusen Hiki;* Chin., *Moxian;* 1846-1920). Dharma successor of Shogan Mokuchu in the Soto lineage of Japanese Zen Buddhism. He practiced Zen under Sengai Ekido, served as the abbot of Eihei Temple, the chief temple of the Soto lineage, and founded the Nittai, Tanjo, and Kogyo temples. He was given the title "Myokan-doki Zenji."

Morita Goyu (*Morita Goyu* or *Daikyu Goyu;* Chin., *Sentian Wuyou* or *Daxiu Wuyou;* 1833-1915). Disciple of Ekido in the Soto lineage of Japanese Zen Buddhism. He was the abbot of Eihei Temple.

Nannin (*Nannin Zengu;* Chin., *Nanyin;* 1834-1904). He belonged to the Hakuin branch of the Rinzai lineage of Japanese Zen Buddhism.

Nanquan (*Nanquan Puyuan;* 748-834). Dharma successor of Mazu Daoyi. He built a Chan monastery on Mt. Nanquan in Chizhou and remained there for more than thirty years. According to traditional accounts, he had seventeen Dharma successors, among them were Zhaozhou Congshen, Changsha Jingcen, and Baima Tanzhao.

Nanta Guangyong (*Nanta Guangyong;* 850-938). Founder of the Nanta branch of the Guiyang lineage of Chinese Chan Buddhism. Dharma successor of Yangshan Huiji. He resided in Nanta near Mt. Yang. Bajiao Huiqing and Qinghua Quancun were his students.

Nanyang Huizhong (*Nanyang Huizhong;* 675-775). Dharma successor of Dajian Huineng. He settled on Mt. Baiya in Nanyang for forty years, accepted an invitation from the emperor to be his instructor, taught the three Tang Dynasty Emperors Xuanzong, Suzong, and Daizong, and was honored with the title "Imperial Master." He was given the posthumous name "Chan Master Dazheng" (Great Attainment).

Nanyue Huairang (*Nanyue Huairang;* 677-744). Dharma successor of Dajian Huineng. He resided at Fuyan Temple on Mt. Heng. Mazu Daoyi was the only one of his six disciples to receive transmission. Two of the five traditional lineages of Chan trace their origins to the Sixth Patriarch through Nanyue Huairang and Mazu Daoyi. He was given the posthumous name "Chan Master Dahui" (Great Wisdom).

Niaoke Daolin (*Niaoke Daolin;* 741-824). Disciple of Jingshan Daoqin in the Niutou lineage of Chinese Chan Buddhism. He resided at Fenglin Temple on Mt. Taiwang, and was given the posthumous name "Chan Master Yuanxiu" (Complete Cultivation).

Qingsu (*Qingsu;* n.d.). Disciple of Ciming Chuyuan for thirteen years. He resided in Lu Yuan in Huxiang.

Qingyuan Xingsi (*Qingyuan Xingsi;* 660-740). Dharma successor of Dajian Huineng. He resided at Jingju Temple on Mt. Qingyuan, and Shitou Xiqian was his Dharma successor. The Caodong, Yunmen, and Fayan lineages of Chinese Chan Buddhism trace their origins back to him. He was given the posthumous name "Hongji" (Great Charity).

Qisong (*Fori Qisong;* 1007-1072). Disciple of Dongshan Xiaocong in the Yunmen lineage of Chinese Chan Buddhism. He resided on Mt. Fori, wrote the *Fujiao Pian* (To Assist the Teaching), and compiled a history of Chinese Chan transmission. Also known as "Chan Master Yongan," he was given the title "Master Mingjiao" (Brilliant Teaching) by Emperor Ren of the Song Dynasty.

Ryokan (*Taigu Ryokan;* Chin., *Liangkuan;* 1757-1831). Disciple of Kokusen in the Soto lineage of Japanese Zen Buddhism. He became disillusioned with the corrupt practices of temple monks, left to live in a small mountain hermitage on Mt. Kugami, did not run a temple, and had no disciples. His humble practice consisted of writing *kanshi* (poems composed in classical Chinese), sitting in meditation, and playing with the village children. Also known as "Magari," he called himself "Taigu" (Great Fool).

Sengai (*Sengai Gibon;* Chin., *Xianyai Yifan;* 1750-1837). Disciple of Gessen Zenne in the Rinzai lineage of Japanese Zen Buddhism. He studied under Zuigan and Bankoku, and served as abbot of Shofuku Temple in Fukuoka, the first Zen temple in Japan. He was known for his calligraphy and humorous ink paintings. Tangen Toi was his disciple.

Shenguang Huike (*Shenguang Huike;* 487-593). Second Patriarch of Chinese Chan Buddhism. Dharma successor of Bodhidharma. He resided at Kuangjiu Temple in Wancheng and transmitted the Dharma to Jianzhi Sengcan, the Third Patriarch of Chinese Chan Buddhism. Also known as "Sengke," he was given the posthumous names "Master Zhengzong Pujue" (Right-Lineage Universal-Awakening) and "Chan Master Dazu" (Great Patriarch).

Shenhui (*Heze Shenhui;* 668-760). Founder of the Heze lineage of Chinese Chan Buddhism. Dharma successor of Dajian Huineng. He promoted Huineng's place in Chinese Chan history and supported the Southern school of Chan. He is a controversial figure whose teachings stressed sudden enlightenment. Wuming Huixing and Faru were among his disciples. He was given the posthumous name "Master Zhenzong" (True School).

Shinkan (*Joa Shinkan;* Chin., *Zhenguan;* 1269-1341). Founder of the Shijo branch of the Jishu lineage of Japanese Jodo Buddhism. Disciple of Ninsho at Gokuraku Temple in Kamakura. He journeyed through the country as a wandering monk, founded Konren Temple in Kyoto, and was supported by the noble figure Kogiin.

Shinran (*Gutoku Shinran* or *Shinran Shonin;* Chin., *Qinluan;* 1173-1262). Founder of the Jodo-shin school of Japanese Buddhism. Disciple of Honen. He became a monk of Tendai Buddhism, abandoned Tendai to study with Honen, was banished from the capital with his teacher, and raised a family after he was pardoned. He authored *Kyogyo Shinsho,* a compilation of passages and commentaries on Buddhist sutras pertinent to Jodo (Pure Land) Buddhism. Also known as "Hannen," "Shakku," and "Zenshin," he was given the posthumous name "Kenshin-daishi" (Great Teacher Who Saw the Truth).

Shuangxi Buna (*Shuangxi Buna;* Song Dynasty). Also known as "Shuangxi Buna Ru."

Tanzhao (*Baima Tanzhao;* n.d.). Disciple of Nanquan Puyuan. He resided at Baima Temple in Jingnan. Huoshan Wuming was his disciple.

Tianhuang Daowu (*Tianhuang Daowu;* 748-807). Dharma successor of Shitou Xiqian. He also studied under Mazu Daoyi, resided at Tianhuang Temple in Jingzhou, and transmitted the Dharma to Longtan Chongxin.

Tosui (*Tosui Unkei;* Chin., *Tiaoshui;* 1613-1683). Disciple of Gantetsu and belonged to the Soto lineage of Japanese Zen Buddhism. He resided at Zenrin Temple in northern Kyushu, and then gave up the temple life to become a beggar when he was over sixty years old. He was also known as "Unkei" and "Unkan."

Weikuan (*Xingshan Weikuan;* 755-817). Disciple of Mazu Daoyi. Also known as "Weikuan of Xingshan Temple in Jingzhao," he was given the posthumous name "Chan Master Dache" (Great Penetration).

Wenxi (*Wuzhu Wenxi;* 821-900). Dharma successor of Yangshan Huiji in the Guiyang lineage of Chinese Chan Buddhism. He was known to speak with Manjusri Bodhisattva.

Wude (*Fenyang Shanzhao;* 947-1024). Dharma successor of Shoushan Xingnian in the Linji lineage of Chinese Chan Buddhism. He traveled extensively and studied with many teachers, then settled and taught at Taizi Temple in Fenzhou for thirty years. The first master to add verse commentaries to *gongans,* his teachings drew widely from different schools. According to traditional accounts, he only had seven disciples; among them were Ciming Chuyuan, Langya Huijue, and Dayu Shouzhi.

Wumen (*Wumen Huikai;* 1183-1260). Dharma successor of Yuelin Shiguan in the Yangqi branch of the Linji lineage of Chinese Chan Buddhism. He compiled a collection of forty-eight famous *gongans* with his own verses and commentaries in a work known as the *Wumen Guan* (*Gateless Gate*). Emperor Lizong honored him with the title of "Chan Master Foyan" (Buddha Eye).

Wuxiang (*Yizhou Wuxiang;* 684-762). Disciple of Zizhou Chuji. He was a member of the Silla royal family of Korea who went to China and became a disciple of Zizhou Chuji. He belonged to the fourth generation of Hongren's Dharma descendants, resided at Jingzhong Temple in Chengdu, and transmitted the Dharma to Baotang Wuzhu. He was also known as "Monk Jin" and "Wuxiang of Jingzhong Temple."

Xiangyan Zhixian (*Xiangyan Zhixian;* d. 898). Dharma successor of Guishan Lingyou. He originally studied under Baizhang Huaihai, awakened upon hearing the sound of a stone hitting bamboo when studying with Guishan, resided at Xianyan Temple in Dengzhou, and composed more than two hundred verses. He was given the posthumous name "Chan Master Xideng" (Harmonious Light).

Xuefeng (*Xuefeng Yicun;* 822-908). Dharma successor of Deshan Xuanjian. He was the attendant of Vinaya Master Qingxuan at Yurun Temple, went to study the Dharma with Master Hengzhao on Mt. Furong at seventeen, attained profound awakening while on one of his travels with Yantou Quanhuo, and founded Guangfu Monastery on Mt. Xuefeng. Yunmen Wenyan, Baofu Zongcan, and Changqing Huileng were among his disciples. He was given the posthumous name "Master Zhenjue" (True Awakening).

Yangshan (*Yangshan Huiji;* 807-883). One of the founders of the Guiyang lineage of Chinese Chan Buddhism. Disciple of Guishan Lingyou. He resided on Mt. Yang. Nanta Guangyong, Wuzhu Wenxi, and Huoshan Jingtong were among his disciples. He was given the posthumous name "Chan Master Zhitong" (Penetrating Wisdom).

Yantou (*Yantou Quanhuo;* 858-887). Dharma successor of Deshan Xuanjian. He studied the Vinaya and Buddhist sutras as a young man, traveled extensively with his friend Xuefeng Yicun, and then settled at Yantou Temple in Ezhou. According to accounts, he was killed by bandits who came to the temple. He was given the posthumous name "Chan Master Qingyan" (Clear Severity).

Yaoshan Weiyan (*Yaoshan Weiyan;* 751-834). Dharma successor of Shitou Xiqian and disciple of Mazu Daoyi. He resided on Mt. Yao. Yunyan Tancheng, Dongshan Liangjie, Daowu Yuanzhi, Caoshan Benji, and Yunju Daoying were among his disciples. He was given the posthumous name "Master Hongdao" (Propagating the Way).

Yulin (*Yulin Tongxiu;* 1614-1675). Disciple of Danshan Yuanxiu in the Linji lineage of Chinese Chan Buddhism. He was appointed imperial master during the reign of Emperor Shunzhi in the Qing Dynasty. He was given the title of "Imperial Master Dajue Puji Nengren" (Great-Awakening Universal-Charity Capable-Kindness).

Yunmen (*Yunmen Wenyan;* 864-949). Founder of the Yunmen lineage of Chinese Chan Buddhism. Dharma successor of Xuefeng Yicun. He first attained awakening under Muzhou Daoming, studied with Lingshu Rumin, served as abbot of Lingshu Temple after Rumin passed away, and finally founded Guangtai Monastery on Mt. Yunmen. He was given the posthumous name "Chan Master Kuangzhen" (Correct Truth).

Yunyan Tancheng (*Yunyan Tancheng;* 782-841). Dharma successor of Yaoshan Weiyan. He resided on Mt. Yunyan in Tanzhou and transmitted the Dharma to Dongshan Liangjie, Shenshan Sengmi, and Xingshan Jianhong. He was given the posthumous names "Master Wuzhu" (No Attachment) and "Master Wuxiang" (No Form).

Zhaojue (*Donglin Changcong;* 1025-1091). Disciple of Huanglong Huinan. He resided at Donglin Temple on Mt. Lu, and transmitted the Dharma to Letan Yinqian, Kaixian Xingying, and Yuantong Kexian. He was also known as "Guanghui" (Vast Benefit).

Zhaozhou Congshen (*Zhaozhou Congshen;* 778-897). Dharma successor of Nanquan Puyuan. He resided and taught at Guanyin Monastery in Zhaozhou. Many *gongans* are derived from his sayings, the most famous of which is known as "Zhaozhou's *Wu*." Yanyang Shanzhao was one of his thirteen Dharma successors. He was given the posthumous name "Master Zhenji" (True Boundary).

Zhengwu (*Yuanzhi Zhengwu;* n.d.). He studied the Dharma under the instruction of Bailian Qian, later asked Huguo Jingyuan for the Way, belonged to Qingyuan Xingsi's lineage, and resided in Tianzhu Temple in Linan.

Zhenjing Kewen (*Yunan Kewen;* 1025-1102). Dharma successor of Huanglong Huinan. A scholar learned in Buddhist as well as non-Buddhist disciplines, he became the abbot of a temple on Mt. Dong and founder of a new temple at Baofeng in Longxing. According to traditional records, Doushuai Congyue was one of his thirty-eight Dharma successors. Also known as "Baofeng," he was given the posthumous name "Chan Master Zhenjing" (True Purity).

Zhichang (*Guizong Zhichang;* n.d.). Disciple of Mazu Daoyi. He resided at Guizong Temple near Mt. Lu and was widely esteemed for expounding Chan. Gaoan Dayu and Li Bo were among his disciples. He was given the posthumous name "Chan Master Zhizhen" (Ultimate Truth).

Zongyuan (*Zhuyuan Zongyuan;* 1100-1176). Disciple of Dahui Zonggao in the Linji lineage of Chinese Chan Buddhism.

Biographies of Other Noteworthy People

Bai Juyi (772-846). Lay disciple of Chan Master Foguang Ruman. An eminent Chinese poet of the Tang Dynasty, he was appointed to a number of official positions and served as teacher of the prince later in his life. He is also known by his style name "Letian" (Joyous Heavens) and "Xiangshan Jushi" (Layman of Fragrant Hill).

Bhiksuni Xuanji (*Wenzhou Jingju Xuanji;* n.d.). She resided at Jingju Temple on Mt. Dari.

Commanding General Li Duanyuan (n.d.). Lay disciple of Chan Master Jinshan Tanying. He served as the prince's teacher during the reign of Emperor Zhezong in the Song Dynasty.

Emperor Dezong of the Tang Dynasty (*Li Kuo;* 742-805). Ninth emperor of the Tang Dynasty and eldest son of Emperor Daizong. He reigned from 780-805. His father was a devout Buddhist who built many temples and shrines. A diligent and frugal emperor, his long reign was one of stability during the middle period of the Tang Dynasty.

Emperor Shunzhi of the Qing Dynasty (*Aixinjueluo Fulin;* 1638-1661). First emperor of the Qing Dynasty. He reigned from 1644-1661 and was greatly influenced by eunuch officials and Buddhist monks. He was also known as "Fulin" and "Emperor Shizu of the Qing Dynasty."

Emperor Suzong of the Tang Dynasty (*Li Heng;* 711-762). Seventh emperor of the Tang Dynasty and son of Emperor Xuanzong. He reigned from 757-762.

Emperor Wu of the Liang Dynasty (*Xiao Yan;* 464-549). Founding emperor of the Liang Dynasty. He reigned from 502-549. A devout Buddhist and an important patron of Buddhism, he took the Five Precepts, received the Bodhisattva Precepts, and compiled *The Repentance of the Emperor Wu of Liang* to liberate the deceased Empress Xi from suffering in the animal realm.

Emperor Xianzong of the Tang Dynasty (*Li Chun;* 778-820). Eleventh emperor of the Tang Dynasty and eldest son of Emperor Shunzong. He reigned from 806-820.

General Cao Han (924-992). A famous general of the Song Dynasty. He conquered the area of Jiangnan during the reign of Emperor Taizu and took Youzhou during the reign of Emperor Taizong.

Han Yu (768-824). A classical prose stylist, gifted poet, and Confucian thinker, he was deeply opposed to Buddhism and Daoism. As one of the leaders of the Confucian attack on Buddhism, he composed "A Memorial on the Buddha's Bones," a vehement appeal for the restoration of the Confucian Way and the suppression of Buddhism.

Head Monk Chu (n.d.). A Chan master during the Tang Dynasty. He resided at Letan Temple in Longxing, Jiangxi Province.

Li Bo (701-762). Lay disciple of Chan Master Guizong Zhichang. He is one of the most renowned and admired poets in China. A diligent reader in his youth, he was influenced by both Confucianism and Daoism. He was also known by his style names, "Tai Bai" (Extremely White) and "Qingian Jushi" (Blue Lotus Recluse).

Prime Minister Pei Xiu of the Tang Dynasty (797-870). Lay disciple of Chan Master Huangbo Xiyun. An eminent Tang scholar and government official, he was one of Huangbo's greatest supporters. He recorded Huangbo's teachings in the *Chuanxin Fayao (Dharma Essence of Mind Transmission)*.

Qin Shaoyou (*Qin Guan;* 1049-1100). A famous poet and writer of song lyrics in the Northern Song Dynasty. He was appointed National Scholar after being recommended to the emperor by Su Dongpo.

Su Dongpo (*Su Shi;* 1036-1101). A poet, artist, calligrapher, and government official; he was one of eight great poets during the period of the Tang and Song Dynasties. His brother Su Che and his father Su Xun were both famous literati. He held several government positions throughout China. According to traditional Chan accounts, Su Dongpo was an eager student of Buddhist teachings and often discussed them with Chan Master Foyin, his good friend.

Su Xiaomei (n.d.). There is controversy surrounding her existence. According to some literary accounts, she was the daughter of Su Xun and younger sister of Su Dongpo. She was said to be as intelligent and gifted as her brothers. However, historical records indicate that Su Dongpo only had an older sister, Su Baniang, who died at eighteen.

Suddhipamthaka (n.d.). One of the Buddha's disciples. He had a dull intellect, and could not memorize any of Buddha's discourses. Knowing this, the Buddha instructed him to cleanse the filth within his mind while doing various cleaning chores. Following that instruction, he later attained great cultivation and eventually arhatship.

Venerable Master Lianchi (*Lianchi Zhuhong;* 1532-1612). Eighth Patriarch of Chinese Pure Land Buddhism. Also known as "Yunqi," and was one of the four great masters of the Ming Dynasty.

Xia Mianzun (*Xia Zhu;* 1886-1946). A renowned scholar, he was highly respected for his work in education. His career in China consisted of teaching in middle schools and teacher training colleges, editing for publishers, writing, and translating.

Xuanzang (602-664). One of four great translators in Chinese Buddhist history. He studied in India for seventeen years and was responsible for bringing many collections of works, images, pictures, as well as one hundred and fifty relics to China from India. The *Da Tang Xi Yu Ji* (*Great Tang Records of the Western Regions*) is one of his most famous works.

Venerable Master Hsing Yun

Founder of the Fo Guang Shan (Buddha's Light Mountain) Buddhist Order and the Buddha's Light International Association, Venerable Master Hsing Yun has dedicated his life to teaching Humanistic Buddhism, which seeks to realize spiritual cultivation in everyday living.

Master Hsing Yun is the 48th Patriarch of the Linji Chan School. Born in Jiangsu Province, China in 1927, he was tonsured under Venerable Master Zhikai at the age of twelve and became a novice monk at Qixia Vinaya College. He was fully ordained in 1941 following years of strict monastic training. When he left Jiaoshan Buddhist College at the age of twenty, he had studied for almost ten years in a monastery.

Due to the civil war in China, Master Hsing Yun moved to Taiwan in 1949 where he undertook the revitalization of Chinese Mahayana Buddhism. He began fulfilling his vow to promote the Dharma by starting chanting groups, student and youth groups, and other civic-minded organizations with Leiyin Temple in Ilan as his base. Since the founding of Fo Guang Shan monastery in Kaohsiung in 1967, more than two hundred temples have been established worldwide. Hsi Lai Temple, the symbolic torch of the Dharma spreading to the West, was built in 1988 near Los Angeles.

Master Hsing Yun has been guiding Buddhism on a course of modernization by integrating Buddhist values into education, cultural activities, charity, and religious practices. To achieve these ends, he travels all over the world, giving lectures and actively engaging in religious dialogue. The Fo Guang Shan organization also oversees sixteen Buddhist colleges and four universities, one of which is the University of the West in Rosemead, California.

Over the past fifty years, Master Hsing Yun has written many books teaching Humanistic Buddhism and defining its practice. Whether providing insight into Buddhist sutras, human nature, or inter-religious exchange, he stresses the need for respect, compassion, and tolerance among all beings in order to alleviate suffering in this world. His works have been translated into English, French, German, Indonesian, Japanese, Korean, Portuguese, Russian, Sinhalese, Spanish, Swedish, Thai, and Vietnamese.

Buddha's Light Publishing
Fo Guang Shan International Translation Center

Venerable Master Hsing Yun firmly believes that books and other means of transmitting the Buddha's teachings can unite us spiritually, help us elevate our practice of Buddhism and continuously challenge our views on how we define and live our lives. In 1996, he established the Fo Guang Shan International Translation Center which immediately began translating his works from the original Chinese into various languages. Centers that coordinate translation or publication projects are now located in Los Angeles, USA; Montreal, Canada; Sydney, Australia; Berlin, Germany; France; Sweden; Argentina; Brazil; South Africa; Japan; Korea; and Thailand. The establishment of these Translation Centers allows for a wider and more rapid distribution of Master Hsing Yun's teachings on Humanistic Buddhism.

To support the work of the Fo Guang Shan International Translation Center, Buddha's Light Publishing was established in 2001 to publish Master Hsing Yun's teachings on Humanistic Buddhism, in the original Chinese and in translations, as well as other important Buddhist works, in their original languages or in translations. In the short time since its founding Buddha's Light Publishing has received several awards for its publications. Best Spirituality Books, Spirituality and Health Awards 2004 was given to *Living Affinity*. *Handing Down the Light*, a biography of Venerable Master Hsing Yun, received an Independent Publisher Book Awards Honorable Mention - Biography 2005. *Tending Life's Garden, Between Ignorance & Enlightenment VI*, received an Independent Publisher Book Awards 2006 - Honorable Mention- Religion.

Buddha's Light Publishing is committed to building bridges between East and West, among Buddhist communities and other cultures. All proceeds from our book sales support Buddhist propagation efforts.

About the Translators

Dana Dunlap has been a Chan practitioner for over twenty years, training in gongan practice with Zen Master Joshu Sasaki in the Rinzai lineage of Japanese Zen Buddhism. He has studied Classical Chinese for over thirty years since he first fell in love with the language at the University of Minnesota in 1969. From 1971-1976, he lived in Taiwan where he studied at the Mandarin Center of Taiwan Normal University. Dana sits in meditation every day.

Pey-Rong Lee has been practicing Buddhism under Venerable Master Hsing Yun for over ten years. She received her B.A. from Claremont McKenna College in English Literature and is an editor and translator for the Fo Guang Shan International Translation Center in Los Angeles.